THE DYSLEXIA BLUEPRINT

NAVIGATING THE WORLD OF DYSLEXIA WITH CONFIDENCE

ADAM MIZDA

INTRODUCTION

From the moment I was diagnosed with dyslexia at the age of six, my educational journey transformed into a challenging adventure filled with obstacles and unexpected turns. It wasn't until years later, amidst the myriad of frustrations and setbacks, that I experienced a profound realization: my so-called disability was, in fact, a reservoir of unique strengths. This pivotal moment wasn't marked by fireworks or a parade but by a quiet, internal acceptance and a newfound hope.

This book is born from that moment of clarity. The core thesis is simple yet revolutionary: dyslexia is not a deficit but a distinctive advantage that offers valuable perspectives. Here, we will explore how what is often seen as a hindrance in school can transform into a powerful asset in life beyond the classroom.

"The Dyslexia Blueprint: Navigating the World of Dyslexia with Confidence" is crafted to enlighten and inspire not only those who live with dyslexia but also their families, educators, and anyone keen to understand the true essence of this condition. Whether you are a parent of a dyslexic child, a teacher, or someone newly diagnosed, this book promises to be a valuable resource. It speaks to both adults and children, those new to the topic and those already familiar, guiding each reader through a journey of understanding and empowerment.

My story threads through these pages, from the struggles of early diagnosis through the challenges of academia to the eventual embracing of my creative and abstract thinking, problem-solving, and rich storytelling abilities. These experiences don't just build credibility; they forge a connection with you, the reader, who might see echoes of your own story in mine.

What sets this book apart is its blend of personal anecdotes, rigorous scientific insight, and actionable advice, all presented with optimism and empowerment.

This book will first help you understand dyslexia, explore daily life with it, and finally, reveal how to thrive because of it. Each section is designed to build on the previous one, providing a comprehensive guide from theory to practice.

I invite you to engage fully with the content, try the strategies discussed, and even challenge some of the presented ideas. Use this book as a launchpad for your journey toward not just accepting but celebrating the unique advantages of dyslexia.

Let us redefine dyslexia together. It's time to see it not as a limitation but as a different way of thinking that opens doors to innovation and success. Remember, you are not alone on this journey. This book is your companion and guide, offering understanding and practical strategies, hope, and reassurance.

Welcome to a new perspective on dyslexia. Let's navigate this path with confidence and optimism.

1

THE FUNDAMENTALS OF DYSLEXIA

D id you know that many of the world's most brilliant minds were once misunderstood? Albert Einstein, a name synonymous with genius, struggled with traditional learning methods during his early education. Like many other historical figures, his unique cognitive style was not a barrier but a distinct advantage that led to extraordinary discoveries. This chapter delves into the foundational aspects of dyslexia, aiming to shift our understanding from confusion to clarity and from seeing dyslexia as a mere challenge to recognizing it as a potential asset.

1.1 Dyslexia Demystified: Beyond the Myths

One of the most persistent myths about dyslexia is that it links to vision problems or a lack of intelligence. This misconception stems from the visible struggles with reading and writing, often misinterpreted as visual disturbances or intellectual deficits. However, current research robustly counters these myths, clarifying that dyslexia is not related to a person's vision nor a reflection of their overall intelligence. Individuals with dyslexia often exhibit average or above-average intelligence. The International Dyslexia Association provides extensive research indicating that dyslexia is a specific neurological learning disability characterized by difficulties with accurate and fluent word recognition, poor spelling, and decoding abilities. These challenges typically result from a deficit in the phonological component of language that is often unexpected in relation to other cognitive skills.

Defining dyslexia is crucial for understanding and support. Dyslexia is a learning difference, not a defect. It involves a distinct pattern of learning, where individuals typically have strengths in areas like reasoning, critical thinking, and creativity, which contrast with their challenges in reading and writing. This definition helps frame dyslexia not as a drawback but as a unique learning profile that requires different approaches to teaching and learning.

Understanding the prevalence of dyslexia is also vital. Studies suggest that about 15-20% of the population has some symptoms of dyslexia, including slow or inaccurate reading, poor spelling, writing, or mixing up similar words. This statistic highlights that dyslexia is not rare but a common learning difference that affects a significant portion of the global population. Recognizing its prevalence encourages a more empathetic and proactive approach in educational and professional environments, promoting an inclusive society where diverse cognitive profiles are acknowledged and valued.

The importance of early detection must be considered. Identifying dyslexia early in a child's life can significantly alter their learning path and self-esteem. Early intervention can leverage the strengths of dyslexic individuals while addressing their challenges effectively, preventing the cycle of frustration and failure accompanying undiagnosed dyslexia. Schools and parents play a crucial role in this early detection. By fostering an environment that looks out for the signs of dyslexia, we can intervene constructively, adapting learning methods that align with how dyslexic individuals perceive and process information.

VISUAL ELEMENT: **Infographic on Early Signs of Dyslexia**

Below is an infographic to aid in the recognition of dyslexia. It visually outlines key signs to watch for in early learners, such as difficulty with rhyming, trouble following multi-step directions, and a tendency to confuse small, visually similar words. This tool is designed to be a quick reference for educators and parents, emphasizing that an early understanding can lead to timely and effective support strategies.

1.2 The Brain and Dyslexia: A Neurological Perspective

Understanding dyslexia requires peering into the most complex organ in the human body: the brain. The differences in the dyslexic brain are fundamental to understanding why reading and learning challenges occur and appreciating the unique strengths and innovative potential of individuals with dyslexia. Unlike a typical brain, where language processing tends to be highly localized, the dyslexic brain uses a more distributed network. This variation affects how phonemes, the smallest sound units in speech, are processed. The struggle often seen in dyslexia, particularly with phonological processing, can be traced back to how different brain areas communicate and coordinate.

Functional MRI studies have shown that those with dyslexia display less activity in the left hemisphere areas traditionally associated with reading, such as the inferior frontal gyrus and the parietal-temporal area. Instead, there is more reliance on anterior regions and right hemisphere processes. This alternate wiring isn't a shortfall—it's a different approach to processing information, which can lead to difficulties with conventional reading and writing tasks but enhancements in other cognitive areas like big-picture thinking, pattern recognition, and spatial awareness.

Neuroplasticity, the brain's ability to form and reorganize synaptic connections, especially in response to learning or experience, plays a crucial role in understanding dyslexia. This adaptability of the brain is a beacon of hope, as it implies that with the right teaching strategies, the brain can develop new pathways that aid in more effective reading and learning. For instance, structured literacy programs that emphasize phonics and multi-sensory learning can reshape the way the dyslexic brain works, making reading and writing more accessible. This ability of the brain to adapt and change offers a powerful counter-narrative to the myth that dyslexia is a lifelong barrier to academic or professional success.

Recent neurological research continues to shed light on the dyslexic brain, providing us with a richer understanding and more nuanced approaches to education and support. Studies utilizing advanced imaging techniques have begun to illustrate how interventions can lead to changes in brain activity patterns, suggesting that targeted educational strategies can significantly improve the reading skills of individuals with dyslexia. These findings underscore the importance of evidence-based teaching methods that cater to the specific neurological profile of dyslexic learners.

These insights into the brain's function and its plasticity are not just academic; they have real-world implications for teaching and supporting individuals with dyslexia. Knowing that the brain can develop new pathways and that certain regions can be stimulated to enhance reading skills informs more effective teaching strategies. For educators, this means adopting approaches that are tailored to the dyslexic brain, such as those that improve phonemic awareness through multi-sensory engagement or that utilize technology to provide customized reading support. For parents and policymakers, it underscores the importance of early screening and intervention, guided by a deep understanding of the neurological underpinnings of dyslexia. By aligning educational strategies with how the dyslexic brain processes information, we can facilitate a learning environment that not only addresses challenges but also plays to the strengths of dyslexic individuals, preparing them for success in diverse fields and endeavors.

1.3 Identifying Dyslexia: Signs Across Different Ages

Recognizing the signs of dyslexia early in a person's life can significantly enhance their learning experience and quality of life. Dyslexia manifests differently across various stages of development, and understanding these variations is critical for parents, educators, and even adults who might suspect they have dyslexia. By identifying these signs, we can provide interventions that cater to each individual's needs.

For preschool-aged children, the early indicators of dyslexia are often subtle but distinct. Parents and educators should look for phonological awareness difficulties, including the recognition of rhymes and the ability to break words into smaller sound units, a foundational skill for reading. Another sign is delayed speech development or mixing up sounds in multi-syllable words. For example, a child might consistently mispronounce "spaghetti" as "pasketti." Difficulty following multi-step directions or learning nursery rhymes and song lyrics can also be indicators. These signs can often be overlooked as simple developmental variances, but it's advisable to consider a deeper assessment when they persist. Recognizing these early signs can be crucial, as interventions at this stage are often more effective, potentially easing the path that lies ahead in their educational journey.

As children enter school age, the signs of dyslexia become more pronounced and are often related to direct learning activities. You might notice that a child struggles with learning the alphabet, connecting letters to sounds, or may mix up letters like 'b' and 'd' or 'p' and 'q.' Such children may also have difficulty remembering sight words that somebody can't easily sound out. When reading, they might guess based on the shape of the word or the context of the sentence rather than reading the word itself. This can lead to significant frustration as their peers progress at reading tasks more quickly. These school-aged children might also struggle with spelling, often spelling the same word differently in a single piece of writing. Observing these academic-based signs clearly cues parents and teachers to consider a formal evaluation. Early and appropriate strategies, such as structured literacy programs, can then be implemented to address these challenges effectively.

In adults, dyslexia is often masked by coping strategies developed over the years. However, specific challenges remain evident, especially in new or high-pressure environments. Adults with dyslexia may find it difficult to process written information quickly, which can be particularly challenging in professional settings that demand fast-paced reading and writing tasks. They might need help with organizing their thoughts on paper, misinterpret figures of speech, or find it hard to learn a foreign language. In the workplace, these difficulties might translate into avoiding tasks that involve extensive writing or public reading. It's essential for adults who notice these patterns to consider a formal assessment. Self-identification can lead to receiving the necessary support, such as workplace accommodations or targeted literacy programs, which can significantly improve job performance and personal satisfaction.

A comprehensive assessment for dyslexia typically involves a series of tests conducted by a trained professional, usually a psychologist or a specialist in educational diagnostics. These evaluations are designed to measure a range of reading, spelling, and phonological processing skills, among others. The process also considers the individual's educational, psychological, and medical history to ensure an accurate diagnosis. This assessment is invaluable as it not only confirms the presence of dyslexia but also provides a detailed insight into the specific challenges and strengths of the individual. With this information, tailored intervention strategies can be developed that leverage the person's strengths while addressing their particular areas of difficulty. For children, this might involve structured phonics programs; for adults, workplace adjustments and assistive technology might be recommended. Regardless of age, understanding one's specific dyslexic profile is crucial in turning potential hurdles into stepping stones for success.

1.4 The Emotional Landscape of Dyslexia: Coping with Diagnosis

A diagnosis of dyslexia can evoke a complex tapestry of emotions, ranging widely from one individual to another. Some may feel an overwhelming sense of relief, having finally found the explanation for the challenges they've faced over the years. This relief can be profound, as it provides a name to their experiences and opens the door to targeted support and resources. For others, the diagnosis might initially bring about feelings of frustration or sadness, stirred by misconceptions about dyslexia or concern about the difficulties that lie ahead. Parents might worry about the challenges their child will face, while adults diagnosed later in life may reflect on years of unexplained struggles and missed opportunities.

Navigating these emotions is a critical step following diagnosis. It is important to recognize and validate these feelings rather than dismissing them. Understanding that it's normal to experience a range of emotions can be comforting. Open conversations with family members, educators, or counselors can provide significant emotional relief and foster a supportive environment. This dialogue not only helps in processing the initial emotions but also in shifting the focus towards the positive aspects and potential strategies for managing dyslexia effectively.

Building a robust support system is pivotal in navigating life with dyslexia. This network can include family, friends, educators, specialists, and peers sharing similar experiences.

For parents, connecting with other families who are dealing with dyslexia can provide not only practical advice but also emotional support. Schools and local communities often host support groups and workshops, which can be invaluable resources. Additionally, online forums and social media platforms offer access to a broader community where experiences and strategies are shared across borders, providing support and understanding around the clock. This community aspect is crucial because it helps individuals and families realize they are not alone in this experience; there is a whole world of people who understand what they are going through and can offer support or advice.

For individuals with dyslexia and their families, maintaining a positive self-image and a strong sense of identity can be challenging. The key here is to focus on strengths rather than limitations. Dyslexia is just one aspect of a person's profile—it does not define them. Encouraging participation in activities where dyslexic individuals can excel can significantly boost self-esteem. This might include engaging in creative arts, sports, or other areas where they naturally shine.

Furthermore, setting achievable goals and celebrating successes, no matter how small, can reinforce a sense of competence and pride. It's also beneficial to educate oneself and others about dyslexia, which can demystify the condition and reduce any associated stigma. Knowledge empowers individuals to advocate for themselves or their children, transforming potential vulnerabilities into points of strength.

The stories of those who have thrived despite their dyslexia can serve as powerful motivation. Consider the achievements of individuals like Richard Branson and

Agatha Christie, both of whom turned their dyslexic thinking into a unique advantage in their fields. These success stories are not just tales of overcoming adversity; they highlight the extraordinary potential of thinking differently. Sharing such stories can inspire those newly diagnosed to view dyslexia through a lens of potential rather than limitation. Teachers and parents can play a significant role by integrating success stories into learning and discussions, cultivating an environment where dyslexic individuals are encouraged to aspire and achieve.

In summary, understanding the emotional impact of a dyslexia diagnosis is as crucial as understanding the condition itself. By addressing the emotional responses directly, building a solid support network, fostering resilience and a positive self-image, and highlighting inspiring success stories, individuals with dyslexia and their families can navigate this aspect of their lives with confidence. This approach helps in coping with the diagnosis and sets the foundation for a fulfilling journey of growth and discovery. As we continue to explore and understand the multifaceted experiences of dyslexia, we open up a world of possibilities for those affected, encouraging them to redefine the narrative of their lives in vibrant and empowering ways.

2

THE STRENGTHS OF DYSLEXIA

I magine for a moment that you are an architect, visualizing a complex structure not yet built, perceiving every detail, every angle with stunning clarity. Now, consider that this ability to think in a rich, three-dimensional way is a natural strength for many individuals with dyslexia. This chapter explores such incredible advantages, unveiling how what is often seen as a learning challenge can also bestow powerful cognitive abilities that are highly valued in many professional fields and everyday life situations.

2.1 Thinking in 3D: Spatial Strengths Uncovered

Many people with dyslexia inherently excel in spatial reasoning, a skill that allows them to perceive, manipulate, and analyze space and shapes. This ability is not merely about understanding geometry or being good at puzzles; it's about thinking in a way that transforms two-dimensional information into multi-dimensional solutions. Spatial reasoning is crucial in fields such as engineering, architecture, and visual arts, where visualizing objects in three dimensions is a daily requirement.

For instance, consider an engineer who must conceptualize how different parts of a machine will fit together and function before even a single piece is manufactured. People with strong spatial abilities are often able to mentally 'see' and rotate these components, understanding how they will interact in a real-world setting. This capability is not just beneficial; it's transformative, allowing for more innovative and efficient designs. In architecture, the ability to envision spaces and structures that are both functional and aesthetically pleasing relies heavily on robust spatial reasoning. Dyslexic architects often describe their process as 'seeing' the completed building in their minds, turning it over, exploring it from all angles before a single line is drawn on paper.

Visual thinking, another strength commonly found in individuals with dyslexia, involves processing and understanding information through images. This way of thinking can lead to success in numerous fields, particularly in the arts. For visual thinkers, information is understood and remembered as pictures, which can be an incredibly powerful tool for creative expression. A graphic designer, for example, might use this skill to create compelling visuals that convey complex information quickly and effectively, capturing nuances that text alone could not. In fields like film and photography, the ability to think in images is indispensable and often leads to groundbreaking work that pushes boundaries and challenges traditional perspectives.

Learning through doing, or experiential learning, is particularly effective for those with dyslexia. This hands-on approach allows learners to engage directly with materials and concepts, making abstract ideas more concrete and understandable. For example, a dyslexic student might struggle to grasp mathematical concepts through numbers and equations alone but thrive when using physical objects to explore these concepts. This method of learning not only reinforces understanding but also builds confidence, as students see firsthand the results of their problem-solving efforts.

ACTIVITIES TO BOOST **Spatial Skills**

To further hone your spatial reasoning abilities, consider engaging in activities that challenge and expand these skills. Building models from kits, such as those for ships, airplanes, or cars, can be an excellent practice. These activities require you to interpret two-dimensional diagrams and translate them into three-dimensional objects, a process that mirrors the tasks faced by professionals in engineering and architectural fields. Additionally, engaging in video games that require navigation and strategy, such as Minecraft or Tetris, can also enhance your spatial awareness and strategic planning skills. These games simulate environments that require players to manipulate blocks and build complex structures, all while adhering to the laws of physics and spatial relationships.

For those who enjoy more tactile experiences, sculpture or pottery can be a wonderful way to develop spatial and visual thinking skills. These art forms require the artist to visualize the final product and understand how the materials can be manipulated to achieve the desired outcome. Each piece of clay manipulated or each angle sculpted in stone can deepen your spatial understanding and artistic expression.

By embracing these activities, you not only enrich your skill set but also turn what might have been perceived as a learning challenge into a profound advantage. Whether in professional fields that value these skills or through hobbies that bring joy and satisfaction, the ability to think in three dimensions can open up a world of possibilities. So, as you engage with these exercises, remember that each step you take is not just about improving a skill—it's about reshaping how you see and interact with the world around you.

2.2 Dyslexia and Creativity: Unlocking Innovative Potential

Creativity often thrives where there is the ability to see the world through a different lens, and dyslexia provides just that—a unique perceptual experience that can lead to high levels of divergent thinking and innovation. Studies have repeatedly shown a correlation between dyslexia and enhanced creative abilities. A fascinating 2018 study from the University of Cambridge found that individuals with dyslexia tend to excel in exploring new possibilities and are particularly adept at tasks requiring the generation of novel ideas. This cognitive flexibility is a hallmark of what we often refer to as 'thinking outside the box,' a vital component in creative and innovative professions.

In the creative industries, dyslexic individuals are not just participating; they are leading and revolutionizing these fields. Take the arts, for instance, where nonlinear thinking helps in visual and performance arts, allowing creators to forge immersive experiences that captivate audiences. Similarly, in fields like graphic design and multimedia, dyslexics often use their ability to interpret and connect disparate visual elements in ways that others might not see. This ability to think differently is also invaluable in roles such as creative direction, where overseeing the visual and conceptual aspects of projects requires a knack for innovative thinking and problem-solving.

Moreover, the realm of literature and screenwriting also sees a disproportionate contribution from those with dyslexia. Here, the ability to craft detailed narratives and complex characters can be aided by the dyslexic thinker's capacity to view the world from various perspectives simultaneously. The narrative depth achieved by such writers often resonates deeply with audiences, offering new insights and experiences. The link between dyslexia and creativity extends to the innovative problem-solving required in entrepreneurship, where identifying unique market gaps and solutions is crucial. Dyslexic entrepreneurs are known for their resilience and ability to think on their feet, turning potential challenges into business opportunities.

Nurturing this inherent creativity is crucial, both in educational settings and at home. Schools can support creative growth in dyslexic students by incorporating more project-based learning, which allows students to engage deeply with concepts and ideas in a hands-on manner. Projects that blend different subjects, like art and science, can be particularly beneficial, allowing students to use their creativity to explore scientific concepts or historical events creatively. At home, parents can encourage creativity by providing a variety of materials and experiences—from art supplies to musical instruments—allowing children to express themselves in diverse ways. Regular visits to museums, theaters, and cultural events can also stimulate creative thinking and appreciation.

Encouraging a creative routine is also beneficial. This might include designated times for drawing, writing, or other creative activities, which help inculcate a habit of creativity. Importantly, it's essential for both educators and parents to foster an environment where creative efforts are celebrated without undue emphasis on 'right' or 'wrong' outcomes. Such validation encourages further exploration and confidence in creative abilities.

Innovative Dyslexics

Highlighting stories of well-known dyslexics whose creativity led to significant achievements can serve as a powerful inspiration for readers. Consider the renowned director Steven Spielberg, whose dyslexia was not diagnosed until he was an adult. Spielberg's cinematic style, characterized by its innovative use of visuals and storytelling, has captivated audiences worldwide, earning him multiple awards and accolades. His ability to vividly portray complex narratives and characters is a testament to the creative strengths that dyslexia can foster.

Another exemplary figure is Agatha Christie, one of the most famous novelists of all time, whose dyslexia did not hinder her from crafting intricate plots and memorable characters. Christie's novels often weave complex narratives that require keeping track of various storylines and details—an ability that her dyslexic thinking enhanced. Her creative legacy continues to influence the mystery genre profoundly.

These stories underscore the potential for individuals with dyslexia to make substantial contributions to creative fields. They serve as reminders that dyslexia, often perceived as a barrier to traditional learning, can also be a powerful driver of creative excellence. By embracing and nurturing the creative potential inherent in dyslexia, we can unlock a wealth of innovation and artistry that might otherwise remain untapped. As we continue to explore the strengths associated with dyslexia, it becomes clear that the ability to think differently can lead to remarkable achievements, reshaping how we understand creativity and who can contribute to its progress.

2.3 Problem-Solving Skills: Dyslexia's Hidden Advantage

One of the most remarkable yet often overlooked strengths of individuals with dyslexia is their innate problem-solving prowess. While traditional educational environments can sometimes obscure this talent, it becomes increasingly apparent in real-world scenarios where unconventional thinking is not just beneficial but required. Individuals with dyslexia possess the ability to view problems from unique angles, seeing solutions where others might only see obstacles. This ability is not just about being different; it's about harnessing a diverse thought process that approaches challenges holistically and creatively.

For many with dyslexia, typical routes to problem-solving do not always align with their cognitive patterns. Instead of following linear steps, they might connect seemingly unrelated dots, leading to innovative solutions that bypass more obvious answers. This capability is particularly evident in dynamic environments where traditional methods fall short, and a fresh perspective is crucial. For example, in emergency situations where quick thinking is critical, dyslexic individuals often excel. Their ability to process information simultaneously from various inputs can be a significant advantage. Imagine a situation in a fast-paced tech startup, where a sudden software malfunction demands a swift and creative fix. A dyslexic team member might identify a solution that others overlook, perhaps by drawing analogies from unrelated fields or by reconfiguring existing tools in a new way.

Moreover, the capacity to think outside the box is a direct result of the dyslexic experience. Schools and workplaces typically reward conventional thinking and rote learning, areas where dyslexics might struggle. However, when it comes to generating novel ideas or reimagining existing systems, dyslexic thinkers often shine. Their ability to think in a non-linear fashion allows them to break away from the norm and innovate. In industries like technology and design, where innovation is paramount, dyslexic thinkers bring invaluable perspectives. For instance, in architectural design, challenges such as integrating sustainable practices with aesthetic appeal often require unconventional thinking. Dyslexic architects might approach such a challenge by integrating natural elements in unusual ways that also support environmental sustainability, thus addressing multiple issues inventively.

Adopting strategies to enhance these problem-solving skills can further empower dyslexic individuals to embrace and apply their unique cognitive approaches effectively. One effective strategy is the use of mind mapping, which helps in visualizing problems and their possible solutions in a non-linear format. This technique allows for the visual arrangement of ideas, making it easier to see connections and opportunities for innovation. Another strategy is engaging in regular brainstorming sessions without constraints. This can be particularly liberating for dyslexic thinkers, as it removes the pressure of right or wrong answers, encouraging a flow of ideas and enhancing creative problem-solving skills.

In addition to personal strategies, creating an environment that fosters and values diverse thinking styles is crucial. Teams and classrooms that include and celebrate different ways of thinking are more likely to benefit from the unique problem-solving abilities of dyslexic individuals. Encouraging open dialogue about diverse thought processes can also lead to greater understanding and better integration of these skills in collective problem-solving efforts. This inclusive approach not only benefits dyslexic individuals but also enriches the problem-solving capacity of groups, leading to more innovative and effective outcomes.

To illustrate the real-world impact of dyslexic problem-solving, consider the contributions of famous individuals like Sir Richard Branson. Known for his dyslexia, Branson's approach to business challenges is characterized by intuitive, big-picture thinking. His ability to cut through conventional boundaries and envision radically different solutions has been fundamental to the success of the Virgin Group across diverse industries. Branson often credits his dyslexia with helping him see solutions where others might not, turning potential setbacks into opportunities for innovation. His ventures, from airlines to telecommunications, consistently demonstrate how thinking differently can lead to extraordinary business achievements.

These examples and strategies highlight the profound impact that dyslexic thinking can have on problem-solving. By viewing dyslexia not just as a set of challenges but as a reservoir of potential, individuals, educators, and employers can unlock doors to innovative solutions that might otherwise remain closed. In a world that increasingly values diversity in thought and creativity, the problem-solving abilities of those with dyslexia are not just advantageous; they are essential. As we continue to explore and embrace these capabilities, the potential for positive change and innovation in various fields is boundless.

2.4 The Entrepreneurs of Tomorrow: Dyslexia in Business Success

Entrepreneurship is often celebrated as a realm where visionaries bring their groundbreaking ideas to life, despite the myriad challenges they face. For individuals with dyslexia, the entrepreneurial journey resonates deeply, as it embodies the essence of turning perceived limitations into powerful strengths. The traits that characterize many successful entrepreneurs—resilience, creativity, and an innovative mindset—are frequently found in those with dyslexia, creating a unique foundation for business success.

Resilience, a critical trait for any entrepreneur, is almost second nature to individuals with dyslexia who have navigated through the educational system and societal challenges. This resilience translates seamlessly into the world of entrepreneurship, where setbacks are frequent and the path to success is rarely linear. The ability to persevere, a skill honed from years of overcoming learning obstacles, equips dyslexic entrepreneurs to face business challenges with a robust mindset. Furthermore, the creativity that often accompanies dyslexia provides a strategic advantage in entrepreneurship. The capacity to think differently, to see connections where others might not, allows dyslexic entrepreneurs to innovate and create unique business models or products that stand out in competitive markets.

Navigating the business world with dyslexia presents a unique set of challenges but also opens doors to distinctive opportunities. One common hurdle is dealing with extensive paperwork and written communication, which can be daunting for someone with dyslexia. However, this challenge also encourages the development of exceptional delegation skills, allowing dyslexic entrepreneurs to build strong teams and focus on their strengths, such as big-picture thinking and strategic planning. Technology, too, offers valuable support, with software and tools designed to assist with organization, time management, and reading and writing tasks. Embracing these tools can significantly streamline business operations and reduce the stress associated with administrative tasks.

Support systems play a crucial role in the success of dyslexic entrepreneurs. Networking groups specifically tailored to entrepreneurs with dyslexia can provide not only practical business advice but also a platform for mutual support and understanding. These groups often facilitate connections with mentors who have navigated similar paths and can offer invaluable insights and encouragement. Furthermore, specialized training programs designed to address the specific needs of dyslexic entrepreneurs can equip them with skills in areas like financial management, marketing, and customer relations, all tailored to accommodate different learning styles. By leveraging these resources, individuals with dyslexia can bolster their entrepreneurial ventures and mitigate some of the challenges they face.

The stories of dyslexic individuals who have launched

successful businesses are not just inspiring; they are a testament to the potential that lies within this unique cognitive profile. Take, for example, the founder of a popular e-commerce platform who utilized his dyslexic strengths to develop a user-friendly website that offers an innovative visual shopping experience, significantly enhancing user engagement and satisfaction. Another example is a tech entrepreneur who, despite her challenges with traditional coding methods, developed a new software that simplifies coding for others with learning disabilities. Her company has not only been profitable but has also contributed to making the tech industry more inclusive.

These success stories highlight the profound impact dyslexic entrepreneurs can have, transforming their challenges into catalysts for innovation and success. As we explore these narratives, it becomes evident that dyslexia, often viewed through a lens of difficulty, can also be a powerful driver of entrepreneurial achievement. This shift in perspective is crucial not only for individuals with dyslexia but for the broader business community, as it encourages a more inclusive and diverse entrepreneurial ecosystem.

In wrapping up this exploration of dyslexia in the realm of entrepreneurship, we see clearly how the traits typically associated with dyslexia—creativity, problem-solving abilities, and a knack for innovative thinking—are also the hallmarks of successful entrepreneurs. This chapter has delved into the ways in which individuals with dyslexia leverage their unique perspectives and skills to navigate the challenges and opportunities of the business world. Through resilience, strategic use of support and resources, and the inspirational achievements of fellow dyslexic entrepreneurs, they carve paths that not only lead to personal success but also inspire change and innovation in the business landscape.

As we transition from understanding the internal strengths of dyslexia to exploring its external manifestations and impacts, the next chapter will focus on practical applications and success strategies that enable individuals with dyslexia to thrive in various facets of life. Here, we continue to build on the foundation of empowerment and potential that dyslexia offers, encouraging you to see beyond the challenges and embrace the vast opportunities for growth and achievement.

3

DYSLEXIA IN THE FAMILY

avigating the waters of dyslexia within the family setting is akin to learning a new language—a language of understanding, support, and shared experiences. As you navigate these uncharted waters, you'll discover the strength of open communication and the power of informed supportive conversations. This chapter is designed to be your compass, guiding you through the essential discussions about dyslexia with your child, helping you to understand their emotions, and providing resources to enrich your family's journey together.

3.1 Conversations About Dyslexia: Talking to Your Child

Approaching the subject of dyslexia with your child is a delicate dance. It's about finding the proper steps to ensure the dialogue is informative and reassuring, and it's crucial to tailor your approach based on your child's age, understanding, and emotions. Initiating this conversation might feel daunting—how do you explain such a complex issue in a encouraging and not frightening way? The key lies in simplicity and positivity. Start by explaining that everyone's brain works differently, and these differences make each person unique and special. You might say, "Just like some people are great at sports and others make beautiful art, some people's brains are fantastic at thinking in pictures or solving puzzles." This approach not only introduces the concept of dyslexia without stigma but also celebrates diversity in skills and talents.

Understanding the emotions your child might be experiencing is crucial in these conversations. Children with dyslexia often feel a sense of relief when they realize there's a reason for the difficulties they've been encountering with reading or writing. However, this relief may be accompanied by frustration or low self-esteem, which stems from previous struggles. Acknowledge these feelings openly and affirm that they are completely normal. Reassure your child that having dyslexia does not define them or limit their potential; instead, it's a part of who they are—an aspect that you both will learn to manage together. Empathy and affirmations can significantly comfort your child, letting them know they are not alone in this challenge.

Fostering open communication is another pillar in supporting your child. Create an environment where your child feels safe to express their feelings about dyslexia, whether it's frustration, sadness, or success. Encourage them to share their school experiences and any new strategies they find helpful. This open line of communication will not only help you understand their needs better and reinforce your role as their steadfast supporter. Moreover, regular discussions about school and learning can help you gauge how well they are coping and adapting, allowing you to intervene with additional support when necessary.

RESOURCES FOR FAMILIES

To further aid your understanding and ability to support your child, numerous resources can be invaluable in your family's dyslexia journey. Books such as "The Dyslexic Advantage" by Brock L. Eide and Fernette F. Eide offer insights into the strengths of dyslexic thinking. At the same time "Overcoming Dyslexia" by Sally Shaywitz provides practical advice on supporting dyslexic children in their academic life. Websites like the Yale Center for Dyslexia & Creativity and Understood.org are also excellent sources of information, offering articles, tools, and community support that can help demystify dyslexia for both you and your child. Engaging with these resources can be a bonding activity, providing both of you with knowledge and strategies to tackle dyslexia confidently.

Incorporating these elements into your family's approach to dyslexia creates a foundation of understanding and support that empowers your child to confidently navigate their educational and personal life. By discussing dyslexia openly, acknowledging and addressing the emotional aspects, and utilizing available resources, you strengthen your child's ability to thrive despite the challenges. This chapter aims to equip you with the tools to enhance communication within your family, fostering an environment where dyslexia is understood not just as a challenge but as one of many qualities that make your child unique and capable in their own right.

3.2 Creating a Dyslexia-Friendly Home: Practical Tips

Transforming your home into a dyslexia-friendly environment is like setting the stage for success, comfort, and growth. It's about creating spaces that not only accommodate the unique needs of someone with dyslexia but also promote independence and reduce the everyday stresses that can accompany learning differences. One effective strategy is to establish specific areas within the home dedicated to reading and studying. These areas should be well-lit, quiet, and clear from distractions that could disrupt concentration. For a child with dyslexia, having a designated space for reading can make the task feel more manageable and less daunting. This space doesn't need to be large—a cozy corner with a comfortable chair, a good lamp, and easy access to books and materials will do.

Additionally, consider the overall organization of your home. Dyslexic individuals often find it challenging to deal with clutter, as it can overwhelm their senses and make it difficult to focus. Simple organizational systems that are consistently used can help reduce this stress. Labeling drawers and shelves clearly and using color coding can also help make objects and documents easier to locate and return, fostering a sense of order and calm.

When considering reading materials, selecting dyslexia-friendly books and tools is vital. Look for books that use a dyslexia-friendly font, which typically means a larger, sans-serif typeface with ample spacing between lines and words. These fonts reduce the visual stress and confusion that often accompany reading for those with dyslexia. Furthermore, graphic novels and books with visual aids can be extremely helpful as they provide contextual clues that aid comprehension and make the reading experience more engaging. Publishers like Barrington Stoke specialize in books designed for dyslexic readers, offering titles that cater to various interests and age groups. Beyond books, consider tools that aid reading, such as colored overlays or reading rulers, which can help dyslexic readers track lines more efficiently and reduce words' blurring.

Integrating technology in the home is another transformative element for supporting learning and independence in individuals with dyslexia. Text-to-speech software can be particularly beneficial, as it allows written material to be converted into spoken word, helping with comprehension and reducing the strain of reading large amounts of text. Educational apps designed to strengthen reading and writing skills in a fun and interactive way can also be very effective. For example, apps like 'Dyslexia Quest' offer games designed to improve memory, attention, and learning skills through adventurous and engaging challenges. Additionally, consider setting up speech-to-text tools on home computers or tablets. These tools allow dyslexic users to articulate their thoughts and see them transformed into text in real time, which can be especially helpful for completing homework assignments or conducting research.

Establishing routines is an essential strategy in creating a dyslexia-friendly home. Routines can provide structure and predictability, which help to minimize anxiety and stress. For a dyslexic child, routines around homework, reading, and other educational tasks can make these activities part of the daily flow, reducing resistance and procrastination. A visual schedule, for example, can be a great tool to help outline the day's activities. This could include blocks of time for homework, breaks, chores, and leisure activities, all illustrated in an easy-to-understand format. It's also helpful to incorporate routines that build skills indirectly related to dyslexia but are critical for overall confidence and independence, such as organizing their space, planning out school projects, or managing time effectively. These skills not only aid in academic success but also in life skills as they grow older.

By taking these steps to adapt your home environment, selecting appropriate materials, utilizing supportive technology, and establishing helpful routines, you create a foundation that not only supports the needs of a dyslexic learner but also empowers them to thrive. This approach to modifying your living space and daily habits fosters a nurturing environment where challenges are met with creative solutions and every family member can feel equipped to succeed.

3.3 Advocating for Your Child: Navigating School Systems

Understanding your child's educational rights is the cornerstone of advocating effectively within the school system. Across many regions, laws such as the Individuals with Disabilities Education Act (IDEA) in the United States ensure that children with disabilities, including those with dyslexia, have the right to a least restrictive environment. These laws mandate that schools must provide accommodations and specialized instruction tailored to meet the unique needs of dyslexic students. For parents, familiarizing yourself with these rights empowers you and equips you with the knowledge to ensure that your child receives the education they deserve. It's crucial to understand that these rights include the ability to request evaluations at no cost to you, the right to disagree with assessment results, and the right to participate in all meetings concerning the development of your child's education plan.

Working effectively with schools is pivotal in navigating the educational landscape for a child with dyslexia. Effective communication with teachers and school administrators forms the backbone of this endeavor. Start by establishing a collaborative relationship with your child's educators. Express your willingness to partner with them and share insights about your child's challenges and strengths. Regular communication, such as scheduled meetings or updates, can help maintain a clear, ongoing dialogue about your child's progress and needs. When discussing your child's dyslexia, be specific about the challenges they face, such as difficulties with reading comprehension, spelling, or writing. Provide examples and, if possible, suggest strategies that have been effective at home or in previous educational settings. This proactive approach keeps you informed and ensures that the educators are aware of and are addressing your child's specific learning needs.

Navigating the specifics of Individualized Education Programs (IEP) and 504 plans is often the next practical step in securing the necessary support for your child. An IEP is a plan developed to ensure that a child who has a disability identified under the law and is attending an elementary or secondary educational institution receives specialized instruction and related services. A 504 plan is designed to accommodate children with disabilities to ensure their academic success and access to the learning environment. To initiate this process, you can request a writing evaluation detailing your concerns about your child's dyslexia. Once the review is complete, an IEP or 504 plan will be developed if your child is eligible. During this meeting, it's essential to come prepared with a clear idea of what accommodations might benefit your child, such as extra time on tests, the use of technology, or the provision of notes. Participation in these meetings can sometimes feel overwhelming, so it may be beneficial to bring along an advocate or a knowledgeable ally who can help you navigate the discussion and ensure that your child's needs are adequately addressed.

Finding external support can significantly bolster your advocacy efforts. Numerous resources and organizations are dedicated to assisting families and children with dyslexia. Local and national groups, such as the International Dyslexia Association (IDA), offer workshops, resources, and connections to other families navigating similar challenges. These organizations can guide effective advocacy strategies, up-to-date information on educational rights, and referrals to qualified educational therapists and tutors specializing in dyslexia. Some organizations also offer training sessions for parents, which can equip you with skills to advocate more effectively within the school system and beyond. Additionally, consider contacting special education advocates or attorneys specializing in educational law for guidance. These professionals can help understand your rights and navigate more complex situations within the educational system.

By thoroughly understanding your child's educational rights, maintaining open and effective communication with school staff, navigating IEP and 504 plans, and utilizing external supports, you can ensure that your child receives the education they deserve and the support they may need for their unique learning needs. This proactive and informed approach to advocacy empowers both you and your child, paving the way for educational experiences that are enriching, appropriate, and above all, inclusive.

3.4 Emotional Support: Building Confidence and Resilience

Navigating the emotional landscape when you or a loved one has dyslexia involves more than just addressing academic challenges; it's about nurturing resilience, celebrating diverse strengths, and establishing effective coping strategies. Resilience, that remarkable ability to bounce back from setbacks, is especially crucial for children with dyslexia who may face frequent academic and social challenges. One effective way to foster resilience is through structured problem-solving activities that encourage children to see obstacles as puzzles to be solved rather than insurmountable problems. This can be practiced by guiding them through the steps of identifying the issue, brainstorming possible solutions, trying a solution, and then reflecting on the outcome. This method provides them with a template for tackling difficulties and instills a sense of agency and control.

Further strengthening resilience involves regular discussions about past successes. Children with dyslexia often experience repeated struggles, which can overshadow their achievements. By maintaining a 'success journal' or a visual accomplishment board, children can see a tangible record of their successes, big or small, reinforcing the idea that they are capable and can overcome challenges. This visual reminder boosts self-esteem and is a motivational tool during more challenging times. Additionally, role-playing various scenarios can equip children with strategies and language to use when encountering obstacles, preparing them for future challenges and reducing anxiety.

Celebrating the strengths and talents of individuals with dyslexia is equally vital. It's important to recognize and value their skills in areas beyond academics, such as music, sports, art, or interpersonal skills. Highlighting these talents can shift the focus from what they struggle with to what they excel in, providing a more balanced self-view and promoting a positive identity. Organize family events or small gatherings where your child can showcase their talents. Whether it's a mini-concert at home, a family art show, or a backyard sports day, these events allow children to shine and be acknowledged for their diverse capabilities, reinforcing their value and competence.

Developing effective coping strategies is crucial for dealing with the frustrations and setbacks often accompanying dyslexia. Techniques such as mindfulness and positive self-talk can be powerful tools. Introducing mindfulness through simple, guided breathing exercises can help children learn to manage stress and anxiety. Just a few minutes a day can make a significant difference in how they perceive and respond to stress. Positive self-talk is another potent strategy. Teaching children to replace negative thoughts with positive affirmations can profoundly affect their confidence and emotional well-being. Phrases like "I am learning and growing every day" or "I can handle this challenge" can help pivot their mindset during difficult moments.

Fostering a sense of community and belonging is essential for emotional support. Connecting with other families navigating similar experiences can provide camaraderie, practical support, and advice. Look for local or online dyslexia support groups where experiences and resources can be shared. Participating in community events or workshops not only broadens your support network but also helps normalize the conversation about dyslexia, reducing stigma. For children, knowing other kids who face similar challenges can be incredibly reassuring and reduce feelings of isolation or difference.

By actively fostering resilience through problem-solving and reflection, celebrating diverse strengths, employing mindful and positive strategies, and connecting with a supportive community, families can build a nurturing environment that empowers children with dyslexia. These strategies equip them to cope with their immediate challenges and thrive in the face of adversity, cultivating a resilient and confident mindset that will benefit them throughout life.

As we conclude this chapter on supporting dyslexia within the family, we reflect on the journey of building stronger, more resilient children equipped to navigate their challenges and thrive because of them. The strategies and insights shared here aim to empower families to create a supportive framework that celebrates diversity, fosters emotional resilience, and enhances the overall well-being of everyone involved. Moving forward, the discussion will shift to practical educational strategies and classroom interventions to further support dyslexic children, ensuring they receive the best possible support in their learning environments.

4

DYSLEXIA IN THE CLASSROOM

I magine a classroom where every lesson and every assignment feels like a key that perfectly fits into a lock, opening up a world of understanding and enthusiasm for learning. For students with dyslexia, the traditional classroom setup can sometimes feel like being given the wrong set of keys. They might struggle to unlock the full richness of the educational experiences offered. This chapter focuses on reshaping that environment, turning the classroom into a space where dyslexic students don't just learn but thrive through the use of multi-sensory teaching methods.

4.1 Multisensory Teaching Methods: A Guide for Educators

Multi-sensory teaching is not just an educational technique but a revelation in the world of learning, particularly for students with dyslexia. At its core, multi-sensory teaching integrates visual, auditory, and kinesthetic-tactile pathways simultaneously to enhance memory and learning of written language. Links are consistently made between the visual (what we see), auditory (what we hear), and kinesthetic-tactile (what we feel) pathways in learning to read and spell. Consider the process of learning new words; a multi-sensory approach would not only involve seeing and saying the words but also writing them out and using them in a tactile way, such as forming letters in sand or tracing them in the air. This method leverages the brain's ability to make multiple connections between these sensory experiences, which can lead to stronger recall and a deeper under-standing of the material.

Implementing multi-sensory strategies in reading, writ-ing, and math instruction can transform the classroom expe-rience for students with dyslexia. For reading, teachers might introduce textured letters to feel the shape of the alphabet while simultaneously pronouncing the sounds, engaging the sense of touch alongside sight and hearing. When it comes to writing, incorporating activities like writing letters in the air with large arm movements before writing them on paper can help encode the movements into memory. For mathematics, using physical objects that students can manipulate—such as blocks for counting or sorting shapes—allows for a tactile experience that comple-ments the visual and auditory learning processes.

Adapting the classroom to support multi-sensory learning involves more than just instructional changes; it also includes modifying the physical environment. Seating arrangements should ensure that every student has an unob-structed view of visual aids and can hear clearly, possibly integrating U-shaped or circular desk setups to foster better engagement and interaction. Visual clutter should be minimized to reduce distractions, and materials should be organized and easily accessible to prevent sensory overload. Additionally, using tools like whiteboards, where visual information can be displayed and explained verbally, can cater to visual and auditory learners.

When assessing dyslexic students, traditional testing methods often do not reflect their true capabilities. It's crucial for educators to find assessment techniques that consider the effort and learning progress, not just the final outcomes. Alternative assessment methods, such as oral presentations instead of written reports or portfolios showcasing a range of work, can provide a more comprehensive picture of a student's understanding and abilities. Feedback should be immediate and constructive, focusing on specific improvement areas while acknowledging what the student has mastered. This approach motivates students and provides them with clear, actionable information on how to enhance their learning strategies.

VISUAL ELEMENT: **Classroom Layout Diagram**

To further aid educators in setting up a dyslexia-friendly classroom, a detailed diagram can be included here. This visual element would illustrate an optimal classroom layout that supports multi-sensory learning, showing the placement of desks, teacher's station, and areas for group activities. It would highlight how such an environment can be organized to enhance learning experiences for dyslexic students, ensuring they are fully engaged and able to access all teaching materials effectively.

By embracing multi-sensory teaching methods, educators can significantly enrich the learning experience for students with dyslexia, helping them unlock their potential in new and exciting ways. This approach not only supports the specific learning needs of dyslexic students but also enhances the educational experience for all students, making the classroom a more inclusive and effective learning environment. As we continue to explore these transformative educational strategies, it becomes clear that with the right tools and understanding, all students have the potential to succeed and flourish academically.

4.2 Tailoring Reading Instruction: Techniques That Work

Regarding reading instruction for dyslexic learners, one size does not fit all. Each student brings a unique set of strengths and challenges to the table, making it essential for educators to adopt a flexible and tailored approach to teaching reading. A foundational element in this personalized approach is using structured, phonics-based reading programs. Phonics instruction involves teaching the relationship between sounds and the letters representing them, which is critical for dyslexic learners who often struggle with phonological awareness. Unlike traditional methods that may emphasize memorization of whole words, phonics teaches the building blocks of words, empowering students to decode unfamiliar words independently. This method is particularly effective because it taps into the logical processing strengths many dyslexic learners possess, allowing them to apply rules and patterns to make sense of reading.

To customize reading instruction effectively, educators must first thoroughly understand the individual learning profile of each dyslexic student. This understanding can be achieved through detailed assessments beyond standard reading tests to explore areas such as phonemic awareness, decoding skills, and reading comprehension. With this information, teachers can tailor instruction to target specific areas of need. For instance, if a student excels in visual learning but struggles with phonemic awareness, the teacher might incorporate more visual aids into phonics lessons, such as using color-coded letters to highlight different sounds. Another strategy is to adjust the pace of instruction, allowing more time for concepts to be absorbed and practiced. This personalized pacing respects the learner's processing speed, reducing frustration and enhancing learning outcomes.

The choice of reading materials also plays a crucial role in the success of dyslexic students. Engaging, dyslexia-friendly reading materials can transform a daunting task into an enjoyable activity. These materials often include books with controlled vocabulary, structured layouts with ample spacing, and supportive visuals that aid comprehension. Graphic novels, for example, can be particularly appealing due to their visual-rich format that supports text understanding. For younger readers, books that integrate interactive elements like lift-the-flaps or textured pages might be particularly engaging. Additionally, incorporating topics and themes that reflect the student's interests can motivate reluctant readers. Whether it's dinosaurs, space exploration, or fairy tales, materials that spark curiosity can encourage frequent reading practice, which is crucial for skill development.

Supporting struggling readers requires an extra layer of attention and resources. One effective approach is the provision of one-on-one tutoring sessions. These sessions allow intensive, personalized instruction to address specific reading challenges in a supportive environment. Tutors can use a variety of methods, from repeated reading for fluency practice to multi-sensory techniques for phonics instruction. Small reading groups also offer significant benefits, providing opportunities for students to practice reading in a supportive social setting. These groups should be carefully composed with attention to students' reading levels and personalities, ensuring a positive dynamic that fosters confidence and learning. In these groups, students can engage in guided reading activities where they read aloud and discuss content in real time, improving fluency and enhancing comprehension and analytical skills.

These tailored strategies in reading instruction are essential for effectively supporting dyslexic learners. By focusing on phonics-based approaches, customizing teaching methods and materials, and providing robust support systems, educators can create a learning environment that fosters success and builds confidence in dyslexic students. As we explore these customized approaches, it becomes clear that the goal is not merely to improve reading skills but to ignite a passion for learning and a belief in one's abilities, opening up a world where reading is not just possible but pleasurable.

4.3 Encouraging Engagement: Classroom Strategies for Dyslexic Students

Creating a classroom environment where every student feels valued and included is more than just a noble goal—it's an essential foundation for effective learning, particularly for students with dyslexia. An inclusive classroom goes beyond merely accommodating these students—it actively embraces diversity in learning styles as a strength that enhances the educational experience for everyone. To cultivate such an environment, educators must foster a culture of acceptance and understanding. This begins with educating all students about the various learning differences that their peers might experience, emphasizing that everyone has unique strengths and challenges. Activities that allow students to explore and celebrate these differences can be particularly effective. For example, projects that require diverse skill sets, such as a class play, can allow students with different strengths to shine—whether it's in crafting scripts, designing sets, or performing. Furthermore, using positive language around learning differences, focusing on 'different learning needs' rather than 'disabilities,' can significantly influence the classroom atmosphere, making it more supportive and empathetic.

Structured group work is another powerful strategy for fostering inclusivity while supporting dyslexic students. When designing group activities, it's crucial to structure them in ways that allow all students to participate meaningfully. This might mean assigning roles that play to each student's strengths—for instance, a student with dyslexia might excel in a role that requires verbal skills or creative input rather than one that demands heavy reading or writing. Educators can facilitate these groups to ensure that tasks are divided equitably and each student's contributions are valued. The benefits of such structured group work extend beyond academic achievements; they also help build social skills and teach students the value of diverse perspectives. Additionally, establishing peer support systems where students can tutor and support each other under supervision can reinforce learning and build a supportive network within the classroom. This not only aids the dyslexic students but also fosters a sense of responsibility and empathy among their peers.

Hands-on learning experiences are particularly beneficial for students with dyslexia, who often thrive when they can engage directly with materials and concepts. This approach, known as kinesthetic learning, involves physical activities that help students understand and remember information. In science classes, for example, conducting experiments rather than just reading about them allows dyslexic students to engage with the material in a tangible way. In history lessons, reenacting events or creating art projects about specific periods can provide context and make the information more memorable. Educators can create an interactive classroom by incorporating games, puzzles, and building projects that cater to various learning needs and styles. These activities make learning more enjoyable and allow dyslexic students to use their problem-solving skills and creativity, often leading to a deeper understanding of the subject matter.

Building confidence in dyslexic students is crucial and can be significantly enhanced by encouraging participation in all classroom activities. One effective method is to provide opportunities for students to showcase their knowledge and skills in non-traditional ways. For instance, instead of a written test, students could demonstrate their understanding through a presentation, a video project, or a series of diagrams. Providing options for completing assignments allows students to choose the method that best suits their learning style, which can lead to greater engagement and better outcomes. Importantly, when dyslexic students participate actively and successfully, publicly acknowledging their efforts and achievements is vital. Positive reinforcement can boost their self-esteem and motivate them to take on new challenges. Additionally, offering constructive feedback privately helps them improve without feeling embarrassed or discouraged. This supportive approach ensures that dyslexic students feel valued and understood, bolstering their confidence and participation in class.

By implementing these strategies, educators can transform their classrooms into vibrant environments where dyslexic students are supported and acknowledged as integral members of the learning community. Through structured group work, interactive learning, and the strategic building of confidence, these students can engage more fully in their education, developing academic skills and a stronger sense of self-worth and belonging. As we continue to explore and implement such inclusive strategies, we pave the way for all students to reach their full potential, fostering a more compassionate and effective learning environment.

4.4 Assessments and Accommodations: Fair Practices

In the educational journey of a student with dyslexia, assessments, and accommodations are not just procedural components; they are vital tools that can significantly influence their academic confidence and success. Understanding and implementing these tools appropriately ensures that dyslexic students are not disadvantaged by conventional testing methods, which often do not align with their learning styles. Accommodations such as extra time on tests, using text-to-speech technology, or providing oral instead of written responses can level the playing field, allowing students to demonstrate their true capabilities. For instance, extra time alleviates the pressure for speed over accuracy, which can be particularly challenging for those who require more time to process textual information. Alternative formats, such as digital texts that can be read aloud by assistive technology, help students comprehend and respond to questions more effectively, ensuring their responses reflect their actual knowledge and not just their ability to decode text quickly.

Implementing these accommodations requires a thoughtful approach that respects the individual needs of each student while maintaining a fair standard for all. This begins with a thorough assessment of the student's specific challenges and strengths, ideally involving input from educators, parents, and students. Accommodations should be based on concrete evidence of the student's needs, such as a psychologist's report or an educational assessment, rather than assumptions about what might be helpful. It's also crucial to ensure that these accommodations are applied consistently across all relevant contexts, from classroom tests to standardized exams. Training for teachers and staff on effectively implementing and monitoring these accommodations is essential. This ensures that the accommodations are used correctly and helps maintain the integrity of the assessment process.

Exploring alternative assessment methods can provide a more holistic understanding of a dyslexic student's abilities. Traditional tests often emphasize speed and memorization, which can disadvantage students who excel in critical thinking and creative problem-solving. Alternative methods, such as project-based assessments, portfolios of diverse work, or verbal presentations, can offer students various formats to express their understanding and apply their knowledge in practical contexts. These methods cater to diverse learning styles and promote skills such as research, synthesis of information, and public speaking, which are valuable in real-world situations. For example, a project-based assessment could involve a student researching a historical event and creating a presentation using a mix of written summaries, visual timelines, and spoken explanations, allowing them to use their strengths to demonstrate their learning comprehensively.

Communication with parents about assessment practices and outcomes is another cornerstone of a fair and supportive educational environment. Transparent communication ensures that parents are informed about the accommodations their child is receiving and the rationale behind specific assessment methods. Regular updates on the student's progress and discussions about the effectiveness of current strategies can foster a collaborative relationship between educators and families. This partnership is crucial for continuously adapting strategies to support the student's learning and development. Effective communication also includes providing parents with resources or training to support their child's learning at home, which can reinforce strategies used in the classroom and provide a consistent learning experience.

These practices of understanding accommodations, implementing them effectively, exploring alternative assessment methods, and maintaining open communication with parents are not just about adhering to educational policies. They are about actively creating a learning environment that recognizes and values the diverse ways students process information and demonstrate their knowledge. By doing so, educators can ensure that all students, regardless of their learning differences, have the opportunity to succeed and be recognized for their true academic abilities.

As we wrap up this exploration of fair assessment practices and accommodations, it's clear that these are not just administrative tasks but are pivotal elements that can significantly influence the educational experience and outcomes for students with dyslexia. By ensuring that these practices are implemented thoughtfully and effectively, educators can create an equitable educational environment that allows every student to showcase their capabilities and achieve their potential. This commitment to fairness and inclusion in the classroom sets the stage for the next chapter, where we will delve into practical skills for everyday success, translating the supportive structures from school into strategies for thriving in daily life.

5

PRACTICAL SKILLS FOR EVERYDAY SUCCESS

I magine stepping into a world where each day feels seamlessly organized and every task, whether big or small, is handled efficiently and confidently. For individuals with dyslexia, mastering the art of organization and time management isn't just about keeping up; it's about setting the stage for personal and academic success. This chapter is designed to transform how you interact with your daily tasks and schedules, offering tools and strategies that align with your unique way of processing information. Through visual aids, technology solutions, and personalized routines, you'll discover how to navigate your day with greater ease and effectiveness.

5.1 Time Management and Organization: Dyslexia-Friendly Approaches

Effective time management and organization can often feel like a juggling act, especially when dealing with dyslexia. However, with the right strategies tailored to your needs, it's possible to turn potential chaos into structured success. Visual planning tools are your first ally in this endeavor. Imagine a large, colorful calendar hanging in your workspace, with each type of activity marked in a different color —blue for school or work, green for personal appointments, and yellow for leisure activities. This method makes your schedule easy to understand at a glance and reduces the cognitive load of decoding text-heavy planners. Similarly, graphic organizers can simplify complex tasks by breaking them into visual components. Whether planning an essay or organizing a project, these tools allow you to map out your thoughts in a way that makes sense to you, making the process less daunting and more manageable.

Breaking tasks into smaller, manageable steps is another cornerstone of effective time management for individuals with dyslexia. This approach transforms an enormous, overwhelming task into a series of small, achievable goals. For instance, if you're working on a research paper, you might break it down into stages like selecting a topic, gathering sources, writing a draft, and revising it. Each step can be checked off on a physical or digital checklist, providing a clear sense of progress and reducing overwhelming feelings. This method keeps you motivated and ensures that you're moving forward steadily, one manageable piece at a time.

Leveraging technology offers additional support, with numerous apps designed to aid organization and time management. For those with dyslexia, task management apps that are visual and user-friendly can make a significant difference. There are apps that allow you to create visual task boards where you can organize your tasks into columns and move them around as they progress. These tools often feature options to set reminders, add due dates, and even share tasks with others, making them excellent for both personal and collaborative projects. By integrating these apps into your daily routine, you can easily keep track of your responsibilities, clearing up mental space for more critical decision-making and creative thinking.

Establishing consistent daily routines is crucial in reducing the cognitive load and increasing efficiency. When you have a routine, you reduce the decisions you must make about when and how to do things. For example, morning routines include specific breakfast times, reading emails, and planning the day ahead. Evening routines involve reviewing what you've accomplished, preparing for the next day, and winding down. These routines act as bookends to your day, providing structure and predictability, which can be particularly comforting when you're dealing with the challenges of dyslexia. Over time, these routines become second nature, enhancing your productivity and reducing the stress associated with disorganization.

Visual Element: Sample Weekly Planner

To help you visualize how a dyslexia-friendly weekly planner might look, consider this sample layout. Each day is color-coded according to the type of activity, with distinct colors for work, personal tasks, and relaxation. The planner includes symbols and icons to represent different tasks, reducing reliance on text and making it easier to understand. This visual approach not only aids in quick comprehension but also makes planning less tedious and more engaging.

Adopting these dyslexia-friendly approaches to time management and organization can transform your daily experience, making it more structured, less stressful, and more successful. These strategies are designed to align with how you process information, providing support where it's needed most and allowing you to focus more on your strengths and less on the challenges of dyslexia. As you integrate these tools and techniques into your routine, you'll find that managing your time and tasks becomes more accessible and more rewarding.

5.2 Reading and Writing in the Digital Age: Tools and Apps

In today's fast-paced digital environment, the ability to read and write efficiently is more crucial than ever. For individuals with dyslexia, this can pose unique challenges. However, the digital age also brings a plethora of tools designed to make these essential skills more accessible. Text-to-speech software, for instance, has revolutionized the way people with dyslexia interact with written content. Imagine listening to the content of an email as naturally as listening to a friend talk or having web pages read aloud to you as you browse the internet. This technology decodes text into spoken language, providing a lifeline for those who find traditional reading slow or painstaking. There are many softwares out there that allow a range of voices and speeds that can be adjusted to suit your listening preferences, turning any text from books to online articles into easily digestible audio.

Furthermore, as we delve deeper into the realm of digital aids, speech-to-text functionality emerges as another invaluable resource. This tool allows you to speak into a device and see your words appear as text on the screen. It's not just about convenience; it's about transforming the writing process into something more intuitive and natural for those struggling with traditional typing or handwriting. There are apps that offer robust speech recognition capabilities that can capture your spoken words with impressive accuracy.

When it comes to specialized reading and writing software, the options are tailored specifically to enhance the learning experience for individuals with dyslexia. These programs often feature dyslexia-friendly fonts, designed to be easier on the eyes, with ample spacing and unique shaping that can help prevent the mixing up of similar letters, a common issue for dyslexic readers. Additionally, the background colors of these programs are often customizable, which can reduce visual stress and make reading a more pleasant experience. Some softwares helps in these ways. It provides advanced spell-checking and grammar tools specifically designed to understand and correct the types of mistakes more commonly made by those with dyslexia.

Turning our attention to educational platforms, it's clear that the digital realm offers a broad spectrum of resources that can transform learning for individuals with dyslexia. These platforms often incorporate interactive elements that make learning more engaging and less daunting. For example, there are learning platforms designed with dyslexic users in mind, offering games and activities that cover reading, writing, and spelling in a fun, interactive way. Other platforms provide audiobooks and literary tools that cater specifically to students with learning disabilities, allowing them to access written material in a format that is more conducive to their learning style. These educational platforms support the development of literacy skills and build confidence and independence, empowering users to take control of their learning journey in ways that traditional educational tools may not.

Integrating these digital tools and platforms into your daily life can significantly alleviate some of the challenges associated with dyslexia. Whether through enhancing your reading experience, facilitating your writing process, or enriching your educational endeavors, these technologies open up a world of possibilities, enabling you to navigate the demands of the digital age more seamlessly and successfully. As you continue to explore and utilize these tools, you'll likely find that they not only support your learning needs but also enhance your overall interaction with the digital world, making reading and writing more accessible and enjoyable endeavors.

5.3 Navigating the Workplace: Disclosure and Accommodations

When you step into the professional world, the question of whether to disclose your dyslexia often becomes a pivotal decision. This choice can influence your experience in the workplace, from daily interactions to long-term career development. Deciding to share details about your dyslexia with employers or colleagues involves weighing the potential benefits and the risks. On one hand, disclosure can lead to access to necessary accommodations that can significantly enhance your work performance and reduce stress. It can also foster a more understanding and supportive work environment. On the other hand, there's a risk of facing misconceptions or stigma associated with dyslexia, which might influence perceptions of your professional capabilities.

When contemplating this decision, consider the specific needs you may have in your job role and the workplace culture. Suppose your dyslexia requires specific accommodations to perform your job effectively, such as extra time for reading tasks or access to specialized software. In that case, disclosing your condition becomes more compelling. In environments that value inclusivity and diversity, you might find a more receptive response to your disclosure, which can ease the process and outcome. It's also helpful to assess how much your dyslexia impacts your daily work tasks. For roles heavily reliant on written communication or detailed reading, the benefits of disclosing and receiving accommodations might outweigh the potential negatives.

Understanding your legal rights is crucial in this process. In many regions, laws such as the Americans with Disabilities Act (ADA) in the United States protect employees with disabilities, including dyslexia, from discrimination in the workplace and mandate reasonable accommodations to support their job performance. These accommodations vary based on individual needs but can include tools like text-to-speech software, additional time for completing tasks, or the option to provide verbal instead of written responses in certain situations. Knowing these rights empowers you to request necessary adjustments and provides a legal framework that supports your discussions with employers.

Advocating for yourself in the workplace is an essential skill that requires clear communication and a proactive approach. Begin by preparing a thoughtful explanation of your dyslexia, focusing on how it affects your work and what specific accommodations would assist you. It's helpful to frame this conversation around the benefits of these accommodations to your productivity and the overall team or company goals. For instance, explain how certain software increases your efficiency or how alternative reporting methods provide more straightforward, more comprehensive insights for team projects. Documenting your needs and the proposed solutions can provide a clear guideline for your employer and help facilitate the implementation of these accommodations.

Success stories of individuals who have navigated workplace disclosure can serve as powerful examples and provide practical insights. Consider the story of a tech professional who disclosed her dyslexia during the hiring process, clearly outlining the tools and strategies that help her excel in her role. Her employer, appreciative of her transparency and the clarity of her requests, provided the necessary accommodations, boosting her performance and setting a precedent in the company for supporting diverse needs. Another example is a senior manager in a multinational corporation who, after disclosing his dyslexia, spearheaded an initiative to improve accessibility resources company-wide, enhancing the work environment for everyone and boosting the company's profile as an inclusive employer.

These narratives underscore the potential positive outcomes of effectively navigating disclosure and accommodations in the workplace. By understanding your rights, effectively communicating your needs, and sharing your experiences, you can create a supportive work environment that acknowledges and actively values diversity in working styles and abilities. As you consider these strategies and examples, remember that the goal is to create a work setting where you can perform at your best, contributing your unique skills and perspectives most effectively.

5.4 Financial Literacy: Simplifying Complex Information

Navigating the world of finance can sometimes feel like deciphering a secret code, especially for those with dyslexia. However, by employing techniques that simplify and visualize financial information, you can gain a clearer understanding and greater control over your finances. Let's explore how you can transform complex financial documents into manageable and understandable pieces. One effective strategy is to use visualization techniques such as charts and graphs, which can turn dense numerical data into visually digestible information. For example, instead of trying to interpret lines of figures in a bank statement, converting these figures into a pie chart can help you quickly see how much you're spending versus saving. Additionally, simplifying documents by highlighting key statistics and summarizing important points in simple language can make them more manageable. Tools like highlighters or digital equivalents can mark important data points or terms in financial documents, making them easier to reference and understand.

Budgeting is a fundamental skill in managing personal finances, yet it can be daunting if you struggle with traditional methods due to dyslexia. Fortunately, some dyslexia-friendly tools and methods utilize visual aids and simple categorization to make budgeting more accessible. Consider using a budgeting app with visual spending categories, such as icons for groceries, utilities, and entertainment. These apps often allow you to see your expenditures in color-coded formats, making it easier to track where your money is going and identify areas where you might cut back. Additionally, setting up automatic categorization for expenses can reduce the need to manually sort through and classify financial information, which can be a tedious and error-prone process for anyone.

For those looking to deepen their understanding of financial concepts, numerous resources, courses, and apps are designed with dyslexic learners in mind. These resources often use clear, concise language and include interactive elements that make learning about finances more engaging. For example, online platforms like Khan Academy offer courses on various topics, from basic budgeting to investing, featuring video tutorials that can help visual learners grasp complex concepts. Additionally, consider apps that incorporate games and quizzes to reinforce financial lessons in a fun and interactive way, which can be particularly beneficial if you find traditional educational materials challenging.

Seeking professional advice is another key step in mastering your financial literacy. It's important to consult with financial advisors who understand the unique challenges posed by dyslexia and can provide personalized guidance. These professionals can help you set up financial management systems that play to your strengths, such as automated tools for regular payments or investments, which can minimize the stress of manual management. When choosing a financial advisor, look for someone patient and willing to explain complex concepts in simple terms, potentially using visual aids or hands-on demonstrations to ensure you fully understand your financial options and decisions.

Navigating your financial life need not be a daunting task, even with dyslexia. By utilizing tools that simplify and visualize information, embracing dyslexia-friendly budgeting methods, learning through specialized resources, and seeking knowledgeable advice, you can gain confidence and competence in managing your finances. These strategies not only help you handle your money more effectively but also empower you to make informed financial decisions that can enhance your overall quality of life.

As this chapter closes, we reflect on the practical skills covered that pave the way for everyday success. From mastering time management to navigating financial literacy, the tools and strategies discussed are designed to empower you, making daily tasks and responsibilities more manageable. As we transition to the next chapter, we'll explore advanced learning strategies that build on these foundational skills, helping you to further harness your potential and thrive in various aspects of life.

6

ENHANCING LITERACY SKILLS

Imagine for a moment that you are an explorer, venturing into the vast and mysterious world of texts and scripts. Each word, each sentence, holds the potential to unfurl new realms of knowledge and imagination. For those with dyslexia, this venture might sometimes seem daunting, fraught with challenges that twist the paths and obscure the signs. Yet, with the right strategies and tools, you can turn these winding paths into a journey of discovery and mastery. This chapter is dedicated to enhancing your literacy skills by navigating and thriving in the world of written language.

6.1 Beyond Basic Phonics: Advanced Reading Strategies

As you grow in your reading journey, moving beyond the basics of phonics is essential. While phonics provides the foundation, advancing your reading skills requires engaging with texts in more complex and dynamic ways. Contextual reading techniques are a pivotal part of this advancement.

These techniques involve using the context surrounding unknown words to infer their meanings. For example, if you come across the word "arboreal" in a sentence reading, "The monkeys at the zoo live in an arboreal habitat," you might not know what "arboreal" means initially. However, by understanding that monkeys live in trees and connecting this to the context of their habitat, you can deduce that "arboreal" relates to trees. This skill not only aids in comprehension but also enriches your vocabulary, allowing you to navigate more complex texts with greater ease.

Speed reading techniques adapted for dyslexic readers also play a crucial role in enhancing your reading fluency. Traditional speed reading methods may not always suit the dyslexic reading style, which often requires more time to decode and comprehend text. However, techniques such as "chunking," where you read groups of words together as a single unit, can significantly increase reading speed without sacrificing comprehension. This method reduces the number of fixations per line, allowing for a smoother and faster reading experience. Practice this by using a pointer or finger to guide your eyes to groups of words, gradually increasing the size of these groups as you become more comfortable with the technique.

Developing critical reading skills is another cornerstone of advanced literacy. These skills involve analyzing the text, questioning its content, and synthesizing the information presented. Start by asking questions like, "What is the author's purpose?" or "What evidence supports this argument?" This approach deepens your understanding and engages your analytical thinking, making reading a more interactive and reflective practice. Summarizing critical points after reading a passage can further solidify your comprehension and retention of the information. Try to distill the main ideas into a few concise sentences, either verbally or in writing, which can help reinforce what you've learned and provide a quick reference for future review.

ADVANCED DECODING STRATEGIES

To tackle more complex texts effectively, advanced decoding strategies that build upon your phonics knowledge are essential. One such strategy is the use of morphology, the study of the structure of words. Understanding the roots, prefixes, and suffixes of words can help you decode unfamiliar words more systematically. For instance, knowing that the prefix "un-" means "not" and the root word "known" refers to something understood, you can easily decode the word "unknown" as "not known." Engage with these components actively as you read, and consider keeping a journal where you can write down new words and break them down into their morphological components. This practice enhances your decoding skills and expands your vocabulary, making even the most challenging texts more accessible.

By embracing these advanced reading strategies, you can transform your reading experience from a task of decoding to one of enjoyment and discovery. Whether you're exploring the depths of a scientific article or the narratives of a complex novel, these skills equip you to navigate with confidence and curiosity, turning each page not just with anticipation of what's written but with the joy of understanding waiting to be uncovered.

6.2 Creative Writing for Dyslexic Minds: Unlocking Expression

Creative writing can often seem like a field strewn with hurdles for those with dyslexia, but with modern technology and structured approaches, these hurdles can transform into stepping stones. Consider the advancements in speech-to-text technology, a tool that has revolutionized writing for many dyslexic individuals. This technology allows you to speak naturally, and the computer instantly converts your words into text. It's like having a scribe in your pocket, ready to jot down your thoughts as quickly as they come. This can be remarkably liberating if the mechanical aspects of writing, such as spelling and grammar, often slow you down. By speaking your ideas out loud, you can maintain your creative flow and capture your thoughts without interruption. There are programs designed to learn from your voice, becoming more accurate as you use them, which means the more you speak, the better they get at understanding your unique pronunciation and speech patterns.

Word processors with predictive text are another technological boon for dyslexic writers. These processors anticipate what you're trying to write and suggest words to complete your sentences, which can be a huge time saver and reduce the frustration of spelling errors. This feature available in certain tools, not only speeds up the writing process but also helps in learning new words and correcting spelling mistakes in real time, reinforcing learning in a practical, hands-on way.

Moving beyond the tools to the structure of writing, structured writing frameworks and graphic organizers come into play as invaluable assets. These frameworks guide you in shaping your thoughts into a coherent structure, making it easier to organize complex ideas. Graphic organizers, in particular, can be a visual lifeline, breaking down the writing process into manageable chunks. They help you map out your narrative or argument visually, making it easier to see the relationships between different parts of your text. For instance, a simple storyboard can help you plan a story, with boxes for each scene and arrows showing the flow of the narrative. This not only aids in keeping your story organized but also sparks ideas for plot developments and character interactions. By using these visual aids, you engage both the creative and analytical parts of your brain, making the writing process more comprehensive and enjoyable.

The art of storytelling itself holds a special power for dyslexic writers. Often, dyslexic individuals possess a rich imagination and a strong ability to think in narrative structures. Tapping into this strength can transform writing from a challenging task into a compelling way to convey ideas. Focus on the elements that make stories come alive—vivid descriptions, engaging dialogue, and dynamic characters. Visual imagery, in particular, can be a powerful tool. By vividly describing scenes and actions, you paint pictures with words, which not only captivates readers but also helps you as a writer to see your narrative more clearly. Engage in exercises that hone these skills, such as describing photographs or paintings in detail or creating backstories for people you observe daily. These exercises not only build your writing skills but also enhance your ability to think creatively and expressively.

Editing and proofreading are crucial skills in the writing process, ensuring clarity and coherence in your work. For dyslexic writers, these tasks might seem daunting, but several strategies and tools can simplify the process. Reading your work aloud is one of the most effective methods. This practice allows you to hear the flow of your language and identify areas where the text may be unclear or awkward. It brings a different sensory experience into the editing process, engaging your auditory skills to catch errors your eyes might have missed. Software tools designed for dyslexics can also be beneficial. There are programs that offer advanced spell-checking and grammar correction tailored to address common mistakes dyslexic users make. These tools provide explanations for corrections, which not only improve your current text but also help you learn and avoid similar mistakes in the future.

By integrating these technologies, structures, and techniques into your writing practice, you can overcome the challenges posed by dyslexia and unlock your full potential as a writer. Whether crafting a novel, composing an essay, or jotting down a poem, the tools, and strategies outlined here equip you to express your thoughts clearly and creatively, transforming the act of writing into an enjoyable and fulfilling expression of your unique perspective.

6.3 The Power of Audiobooks and Podcasts in Learning

Exploring the world of auditory learning opens up a treasure trove of resources that can significantly enhance the educational experience for individuals with dyslexia. Audiobooks and podcasts, in particular, stand out as powerful tools that transform how information is consumed. For many with dyslexia, reading traditional texts can be laborious, fraught with frustration and fatigue. However, when the same content is delivered through audio, it bypasses many of the challenges associated with reading, allowing for a more accessible and engaging learning experience. The auditory format plays to the strengths of dyslexic learners, who often have strong listening skills and can process spoken information effectively. This mode of learning not only makes content more accessible but also adds an element of enjoyment, turning a potential chore into a pleasant and rewarding activity.

The benefits of audiobooks and podcasts are manifold:

They enhance word recognition and vocabulary. Hearing words pronounced correctly and used in context helps solidify understanding and retention. This exposure is crucial for building a robust vocabulary, an essential tool in both academic and everyday communication.

Audiobooks and podcasts can significantly improve comprehension skills. As you listen, you can pause, rewind, and replay sections of the content at your own pace, a luxury that fosters deeper understanding without the pressure of keeping up with text on a page.

The narrative and conversational styles common in audiobooks and podcasts often make complex ideas more relatable and easier to digest, especially when the speaker uses expressive tones and dynamic pacing to emphasize key points.

When curating a learning library of audiobooks and podcasts, it's important to select resources that align with your educational goals and capture your personal interests. Start by identifying your learning objectives—whether it's improving your knowledge in a specific academic field, enhancing your general knowledge, or developing a new skill. Then, seek out audiobooks and podcasts that are not only informative but also engaging. Consider the hosts and narrators—pleasant and expressive voices can significantly enhance your listening experience. Additionally, look for content that is structured to support learning; for instance, audiobooks that are clearly segmented into chapters or podcasts that summarize key points at the end of each episode can be particularly helpful for retention and review.

Integrating audiobooks and podcasts into your daily routine can be seamlessly done with a bit of planning. One of the most effective ways to incorporate auditory learning is by utilizing times when you are physically occupied but mentally available, such as during commutes, while exercising, or when performing household chores. These are perfect opportunities to listen to a podcast episode or a chapter of an audiobook. Portable and accessible from various devices, these resources can turn otherwise mundane activities into productive learning sessions. Moreover, setting aside specific times for auditory learning, such as during a morning walk or evening relaxation, can help establish a routine that enhances consistent learning habits.

Using auditory learning as a supplement to traditional learning methods can profoundly impact your educational journey. For complex subjects that require detailed understanding, listening to an explanatory podcast before reading the textbook can provide a clearer overview and set a strong foundation for deeper learning. Similarly, for literature studies, listening to an audiobook before analyzing the text can help you grasp the narrative flow and character nuances more intuitively. This dual approach reinforces the material through different sensory channels and caters to different learning preferences, enhancing overall comprehension and retention.

In embracing the auditory learning format, you unlock a

versatile and effective tool that complements traditional learning methods, making education not only more accessible but also more enjoyable. As you explore the vast array of audiobooks and podcasts available, you equip yourself with valuable resources that support your learning needs, cater to your interests, and fit into your lifestyle, allowing you to optimize your educational experiences and achieve your learning goals with confidence and pleasure.

6.4 Visual Thinking: Using Mind Maps and Graphic Organizers

Visual thinking strategies, such as mind mapping and using graphic organizers, are not merely tools; they are gateways to unlocking the potential of the dyslexic mind. The concept of mind mapping involves creating a diagram that visually outlines information. At its core, a mind map starts with a central idea, and from this central idea, branches spread out to list major themes or subtopics. Additional details branch off these themes, forming a tree-like structure. This method leverages the dyslexic strength of thinking in images and patterns, making it easier to visualize and remember information. The benefits of mind mapping are manifold—it enhances your ability to plan, brainstorm, summarize, and recall information, making it a versatile tool for both academic and professional settings.

Creating effective graphic organizers also plays a crucial role in visual thinking. These tools can vary from simple Venn diagrams to complex flowcharts, but all serve to break down information into manageable, interconnected parts. When planning essays or projects, a graphic organizer acts as a visual blueprint. It allows you to plot out the structure of your work, ensuring that you cover all necessary points and maintain logical progression. For instance, using a flowchart can help map out the steps of a scientific experiment or the progression of an event in history, providing a clear overview of the sequence and relationship between different elements. The key to creating effective graphic organizers lies in their simplicity and clarity—ensure that each part is clearly labeled and that the connections between different sections are easy to follow.

In digital tools, several software options significantly enhance the process of creating and using mind maps and graphic organizers. Some programs offer robust platforms that allow dynamic and customizable mind maps, suitable for everything from simple brainstorming sessions to complex project management. These tools often feature options to add colors, icons, and even links, making your mind maps more visually engaging and informative. Other tools provide versatile templates for creating various graphic organizers, from timelines to comparative charts, which can be invaluable in planning and presenting information.

Case Studies: Success Through Visual Thinking

The impact of visual thinking strategies in real-life scenarios is profound and inspiring. Consider the case of a university student with dyslexia who struggled with organizing her thoughts for written assignments. By using mind mapping software, she could visually lay out her essays, which helped her see the main points and supporting details clearly. This not only improved her writing structure but also reduced the time she spent organizing her thoughts, allowing more time for research and writing. Another example is a professional in a corporate setting who used graphic organizers to plan and execute projects. By creating detailed flowcharts for each project phase, he communicated tasks and objectives clearly to his team, enhancing collaboration and efficiency.

These case studies underscore the transformative power of visual thinking tools in helping individuals with dyslexia navigate academic and professional challenges. By adopting these strategies, you can enhance your ability to organize information, improve your memory and comprehension, and express your ideas more coherently. Whether you are a student preparing for an exam, a writer outlining a novel, or a professional managing a project, mind maps, and graphic organizers can provide the clarity and structure needed to succeed.

As we conclude this exploration of advanced literacy skills, it's clear that the strategies discussed—ranging from advanced reading techniques to creative writing tools and now visual thinking methods—equip you with a comprehensive toolkit to enhance your learning and expression. These techniques not only mitigate the challenges associated with dyslexia but also leverage the unique strengths it can offer, turning potential obstacles into opportunities for growth and innovation. As you continue to apply these skills, remember that each tool and strategy is a stepping stone towards not just academic and professional success but also personal fulfillment and confidence in your abilities to navigate the world of literacy.

7

TECHNOLOGY AND DYSLEXIA

I magine you're embarking on an expedition in a dense, unfamiliar jungle. Every tool and equipment you choose for your journey can make the difference between forging ahead with confidence or struggling to find your path. For individuals with dyslexia, navigating the dense jungle of written words and complex information can feel just as daunting. However, the right technological tools, like text-to-speech software, can illuminate the path, transforming the daunting into the doable and the perplexing into the possible. This chapter delves into how technology, particularly text-to-speech software, acts as a crucial ally, guiding you through the textual jungles with ease and efficiency.

7.1 Text-to-Speech Software: A User's Guide

Choosing the Right Software

Selecting the best text-to-speech software is akin to choosing the best hiking gear; the right choice can significantly enhance your journey. When you're considering different text-to-speech options, think about the features that are most important to you. Voice quality is paramount —software that offers a range of voices, including different accents and genders, can make the listening experience more enjoyable and personalized. Look for software that allows for voice speed adjustments so you can listen at a comfortable pace for your processing needs. Customization options are also crucial; adjusting the pitch, volume, and even the pronunciation of certain words can help tailor the listening experience to suit your preferences. It's also wise to consider the compatibility of the software with other applications you use frequently, such as web browsers, PDF readers, and word processors, ensuring seamless integration into your daily tech use.

Integrating Software into Daily Life

Incorporating text-to-speech software into your daily routine can revolutionize how you interact with written content. Start by using the software to read aloud your emails each morning. This can help you process your inbox more efficiently, turning a potentially time-consuming task into a more manageable, listenable experience. Use it to read documents before meetings or classes, transforming your preparation process by allowing you to absorb information through listening, which can be significantly faster and less exhausting than reading. For leisure reading, text-to-speech can turn any text into an audiobook, enabling you to enjoy novels, newspapers, or online articles without the strain of reading text. Many text-to-speech tools also offer mobile apps, which means you can take this technology with you on your smartphone or tablet, turning travel time or even workout sessions into productive and enjoyable learning opportunities.

Learning and Productivity Benefits

The advantages of using text-to-speech software extend far beyond convenience. For learners with dyslexia, this technology can be transformative. It levels the playing field by providing access to written information in an auditory format, which can be crucial for those who process auditory information more effectively than visual. This method of consuming text can enhance comprehension and retention of information, as listening can be less tiring than reading, allowing you to engage with the material for more extended periods and with greater focus. Additionally, text-to-speech can boost productivity by enabling multitasking; you can listen to reports or books while engaging in other activities, such as taking notes or even performing household tasks. This efficient use of time can clear up hours in your week, which can be redirected toward other goals and tasks.

Customization Tips

Tailoring text-to-speech software to your specific needs is key to optimize your use of text-to-speech software. Most software allows you to save customized settings, which means you can set up different profiles for different types of text. For example, you might prefer one voice speed for detailed study materials and a faster speed for casual reading. Experiment with different voices and settings to find what feels most natural and comfortable to your ear. Some advanced software even allows you to adjust the pronunciation of certain words, which can be particularly useful if you frequently use texts with specialized vocabulary or names. Don't hesitate to use the help or tutorial features offered by most text-to-speech software to explore full customization options—these tools are designed to make your reading experience as easy and enjoyable as possible.

In embracing these technologies, you're not just equipping yourself with a tool; you're unlocking a new way to experience and interact with the written word. Text-to-speech software offers a bridge across the challenges of dyslexia, opening up a world of possibilities for education, work, and personal growth. As you integrate this technology into your life, you may find that it brings greater understanding and efficiency and a renewed joy and confidence in your interactions with text.

7.2 Educational Apps for Dyslexia: What Really Works

When exploring the digital landscape for tools that cater to learning needs, especially for those with dyslexia, selecting the right educational apps can be as critical as choosing the right kind of physical classroom environment. The criteria for evaluating these apps go beyond just attractive interfaces or popularity; they delve into the effectiveness of their pedagogical approaches, the inclusivity of their design, and the real-world applicability of their features. Firstly, consider the user reviews, which often provide insights into how other users with similar learning challenges have benefited from the app. These reviews can highlight issues or successes that aren't immediately obvious from the app description or initial use, such as long-term engagement levels and any recurring technical problems.

Moreover, the pedagogical foundation of an educational app is paramount. An app designed with a deep understanding of dyslexic learners' needs should offer features like customizable text sizes, choices of fonts, and background colors to mitigate common reading challenges associated with dyslexia. The content should be structured to allow for incremental learning, with concepts broken down into manageable, clear segments that are easy to digest and retain. Additionally, multimodal content, such as the integration of text, audio, and visual aids, can greatly enhance comprehension and retention for dyslexic learners, catering to various learning preferences and needs.

Accessibility features are also crucial in evaluating the effectiveness of educational apps for dyslexia. These features could include speech-to-text capabilities, audio descriptions of visual elements, and easy navigation that does not rely heavily on text-based instructions. Such features ensure that all learners, regardless of their level of dyslexia, can navigate the app effectively and benefit from its content without unnecessary frustration or the need for frequent external assistance.

There are apps that gamify learning to assess and build memory, attention, and processing skills through fun and engaging challenges that are particularly suited to young learners. For older students and adults, there are apps that offer advanced text editing and writing assistance specifically designed for those with dyslexia and dysgraphia, helping users produce clear text. Some tools are specifically designed to assist with math by providing a virtual piece of graph paper where users can set out math problems in a grid, helping to keep numbers in columns and reducing the common transpositional errors that can occur in hand-written math.

Incorporating these apps into personalized learning strategies requires thoughtful integration into your daily or weekly study routines. For instance, setting specific times for app-based learning activities can help create a routine that fosters habit formation and improves engagement. Pairing app sessions with specific goals, such as mastering a new set of vocabulary words or solving a set of mathematical problems, can also enhance motivation and provide clear targets to work towards. Moreover, many educational apps offer settings that allow customization according to individual learning speeds and difficulty levels, making it possible to adjust the learning environment to match personal progress and challenges.

Monitoring progress through app-based analytics and feedback is essential for adjusting learning strategies and ensuring that the apps are meeting the educational needs of the user. Most sophisticated educational apps provide detailed feedback on user performance, highlighting strengths and areas for improvement. Regular review of this feedback can help you understand your learning patterns, including which times of day you are most alert and which types of content you find most challenging. This information is invaluable for tailoring your learning experiences to maximize personal educational growth. Additionally, sharing this data with educators or tutors can help them provide more targeted support in line with your specific learning needs, ensuring that every educational interaction is as effective as possible.

By thoughtfully selecting, integrating, and monitoring

educational apps tailored for dyslexic learners, you can transform your approach to learning, making it more engaging, effective, and aligned with your strengths and challenges. This proactive approach enhances academic performance and builds confidence and independence, empowering you to take control of your educational journey and achieve your full potential.

7.3 ORGANIZATIONAL TOOLS: Managing Tasks and Time

In the bustling rhythm of daily life, keeping track of tasks, appointments, and deadlines can sometimes feel like navigating through a thick fog. For individuals with dyslexia, this challenge is often intensified due to difficulties with traditional note-taking and calendar management. However, the advent of digital planners and calendars has brought a new level of clarity and accessibility, transforming how tasks are organized and managed. These tools are designed not only to keep you aligned with your daily responsibilities but also to enhance the way you interact with your schedules and to-do lists through user-friendly and visually appealing interfaces.

For those seeking the best digital planners and calendars, the focus should be on applications that offer clear, visually structured layouts and customization options that cater to the unique needs of dyslexic users. Visual elements such as color coding, simple icons, and drag-and-drop functionalities can significantly enhance usability. These digital tools assist in keeping your schedules organized and reduce the cognitive load associated with planning and time management, allowing you to focus more on the tasks at hand rather than on how to manage them.

Task management apps are another cornerstone of effective organizational strategy, especially for those who thrive on structure and reminders. Apps incorporating gamification elements can transform mundane task management into a more engaging and rewarding experience. There is an app that turns your daily tasks into a role-playing game, where completing tasks earns you points and rewards, motivating you to stay on track in a fun and interactive way. Another app uses a card-based system that allows you to visually organize tasks into columns and move them across different stages of completion, which can be incredibly satisfying and clear. These apps often include features like reminders, which can be set to alert you of deadlines or upcoming tasks, ensuring that nothing slips through the cracks. By utilizing these gamified and visually oriented tools, you can make task management an integral and enjoyable part of your daily routine, reducing stress and enhancing productivity.

Setting realistic and achievable goals is crucial in effective time management and task completion. For individuals with dyslexia, breaking larger tasks into smaller, manageable steps is particularly important. This approach makes the task less daunting and provides clear markers of progress, which can be incredibly motivating. When using organizational tools, start by defining the ultimate goal and then work backward to identify all the necessary steps to achieve it. There is an app out there that is excellent for this purpose, as they allow you to create projects and then break them down into individual tasks, each with its deadline and subtasks if needed. This method of setting goals ensures that each step is actionable and time-bound, providing a clear roadmap towards achieving your larger objectives.

In mastering time management techniques tailored for dyslexic individuals, the focus should be minimizing distractions and maximizing focus. Creating a dedicated workspace that doesn't have clutter and unnecessary distractions can help maintain concentration. Additionally, techniques such as the Pomodoro Technique, which involves working in concentrated bursts of time followed by short breaks, can be highly effective. This method helps maintain high levels of focus while providing regular breaks to rest and reset, which is important for managing cognitive load.

By embracing digital organizational tools and strategic approaches to task and time management, you can navigate your daily responsibilities with greater ease and confidence. Whether it's through visually appealing digital calendars, engaging task management apps, structured goal-setting techniques, or focused time management strategies, these tools offer pathways to enhanced productivity and reduced stress, allowing you to focus more on achieving your goals and less on the challenges of organization.

7.4 Customizing Learning: Software and Settings for Success

When you think about tailoring a learning environment, it's akin to setting up a workspace where every tool and feature is adjusted to your comfort and efficiency. For students with dyslexia, customizing software settings is not just about comfort—it's about creating a setup that significantly enhances the ability to learn and process information. Let's start by diving into how you can personalize these settings for optimal learning. The first step is adjusting the text display, which can profoundly impact readability. Most educational software allows you to modify text size, font style, and background color. For instance, increasing the text size can reduce strain on your eyes, and certain fonts are designed to increase readability for those with dyslexia. Experiment with background colors; softer hues like cream or pale blue can minimize glare and contrast, making it easier to focus on the text.

As you adapt these visual elements, consider your educational software's audio settings. Many programs offer features that allow you to adjust the speed and pitch of audio playback, which can be crucial if you rely on text-to-speech functions. Slow down the narration if you need more time to process spoken words, or speed it up if you're comfortable with a quicker pace. Customizing these settings to match your learning pace can transform your educational experience, making learning more adaptable to your needs.

Exploring learning management systems (LMS) further opens up avenues for a tailored educational journey. These platforms are invaluable for dyslexic students because they often provide options to customize how content is presented. For example, some LMS platforms allow you to choose how material is displayed, whether in text, audio, or video formats. This means you can select the mode of learning that best suits your processing style at any given time. Additionally, these systems usually support integrating various assistive technologies, ensuring that all tools work seamlessly together to provide a cohesive learning experience. By utilizing an LMS, you can access a wide array of learning resources in formats that are best suited to your individual needs, ensuring that you are not only absorbing information but truly engaging with it.

When discussing educational software features, there are

several key functionalities to consider that can significantly enhance learning for students with dyslexia. Look for software that includes audio feedback, which can reinforce learning by providing immediate verbal responses to your actions, helping to solidify concepts and correct mistakes in real-time. Interactive elements such as quizzes or drag-and-drop activities can also be highly beneficial, making learning active and engaging rather than passive and laborious. Furthermore, features like progress tracking can be incredibly motivating, as they allow you to see your advancements over time, providing a visual representation of your learning journey and helping you identify areas that need more focus.

Transitioning to adapting devices for learning, consider how tablets, smartphones, and computers can be set up to support your educational needs. Most modern devices come with built-in accessibility features that are particularly useful for dyslexic learners. For instance, you can activate text-to-speech functions to have texts read aloud, helping you process written information via auditory means. Adjust the settings to highlight spoken words, which can help link the auditory and visual aspects of reading. Screen filters or overlays can also adjust color contrasts, reducing visual stress and making screens easier to view for extended periods. Keyboard shortcuts can be customized to create quicker access to frequently used functions, reducing the cognitive load in navigating software. By setting up your devices to complement your learning preferences, you transform them into powerful tools that bridge the gap between your potential and your performance.

In embracing these technologies and customizations, you not only make learning more accessible but also more aligned with your unique way of processing information. These adjustments ensure that your educational tools are not just passive elements but active participants in your learning process, tuned to your specific needs and preferences. As you continue to explore and implement these personalized settings and features, you will likely discover that they not only compensate for the challenges posed by dyslexia but also enhance your overall learning experience, enabling you to engage with educational content more effectively and with greater confidence.

As we wrap up this exploration of customizing learning through technology, it becomes clear that the right tools, settings, and approaches can significantly enhance the educational experiences of individuals with dyslexia. By personalizing software, utilizing adaptive learning management systems, and configuring devices to meet specific learning needs, technology can transform from a barrier into a powerful enabler, opening up new possibilities for learning and growth. This chapter highlights the practical steps for individual adaptation and underscores the broader theme of empowerment through technology, setting the stage for the next chapter where we will explore social and emotional well-being in the context of dyslexia.

8

SOCIAL AND EMOTIONAL WELL-BEING

Imagine you're at a lively party or a bustling school event. The room buzzes with chatter and laughter, a cacophony of conversations that seem to flow effortlessly around you. But for you, the scene feels like navigating a maze without a map, where every social interaction is a puzzle you're racing to solve. This is often the reality for individuals with dyslexia, where social settings can morph into challenging arenas, not just because of the noisy environment but because the rapid pace of verbal exchanges can be daunting. Here, we delve into the social dimensions of dyslexia, where understanding nuances and keeping pace in conversations can feel as intricate as reading fine print.

8.1 Dyslexia and Social Skills: Navigating Friendships

In the spectrum of daily interactions, you might find that social cues and quick exchanges, which are effortless for some, require a herculean effort on your part. Misunderstandings can arise when you need a moment longer to process spoken words or when you misinterpret a fast-paced joke. These moments can accumulate, creating a barrier that might discourage you from diving into social waters. However, recognizing these challenges is the first step towards navigating them more effectively.

Developing strategies to enhance your social skills involves a blend of preparation and practice. Start by embracing scenarios that you find challenging. If keeping up in group conversations is a struggle, focus on engaging one-on-one where the pace might be slower and more manageable. In these settings, practice active listening—concentrate intently on the speaker, nodding and responding to show engagement, which can also buy you time to process the conversation. Over time, this practice can build your confidence and ease your participation in larger groups.

Building confidence in social interactions also hinges on accepting and understanding your communication style. Recognize that your contributions to conversations are valuable—even if they arrive a beat later. Prepare talking points before attending social events; this can relieve the pressure of thinking on your feet and help you engage more confidently. Additionally, cultivating interests and hobbies that you're passionate about can provide common ground for conversations. Whether it's a sport, a craft, or a book genre, shared interests are social bridges, making it easier to connect with others.

Interactive Element: Journaling Prompts for Reflection

Reflect on a recent social situation that was challenging. What made it difficult?

List some interests or hobbies you feel confident

discussing. How can these be woven into your social interactions?

Think of a time when you felt misunderstood in a conversation. What would you do differently if given another chance?

Moreover, seeking supportive communities where your differences are accepted and valued can be transformative. These communities, whether online or in person, offer a sanctuary where the nuances of dyslexia are understood and shared. Engaging in forums, local clubs, or social groups centered around dyslexia can provide support and strategies for those who navigate similar challenges. These groups often celebrate diverse thinking styles, offering a reminder that different does not mean less and that every social interaction is a step toward broader understanding and acceptance.

Fostering these skills and environments equips you to manage and thrive in social landscapes. The strategies and mindsets developed here extend beyond mere conversation —they enhance empathy, deepen connections, and broaden your social horizons. So, as you step into your next social gathering, remember that each word, each interaction, is a thread in the richer tapestry of your social world, woven with understanding, patience, and resilience.

8.2 Overcoming Anxiety: Strategies for Confidence

Navigating through life with dyslexia often involves confronting a series of challenges that can stir a whirlpool of anxiety, particularly in environments where performance is measured, like schools and workplaces. For many, the persistent difficulty in managing tasks that others handle easily can lead to a persistent sense of inadequacy and stress. This anxiety isn't just a fleeting worry; it's an intense experience that can affect every reading challenge and spoken interaction. Understanding this connection deepens our comprehension of why tailored support is not just helpful but necessary.

Managing this anxiety effectively begins with recognizing its triggers. In academic settings, the fear of underperforming on a timed test or the apprehension of reading aloud can heighten stress. At the same time, professional environments might provoke anxiety through tasks that require detailed written communication or rapid information processing. Acknowledging these situations as potential anxiety triggers is the first step in crafting a proactive plan to address them. Techniques such as deep breathing exercises or guided imagery can serve as immediate tools to help reduce feelings of anxiety when they arise. For instance, before a stressful meeting or exam, taking a moment to close your eyes and take several deep, controlled breaths can significantly calm the nervous system and clear the mind, making it easier to focus on the task at hand.

Incorporating regular physical exercise into your routine also plays a crucial role in managing anxiety. Physical activities, whether it's a brisk walk, a run, or a yoga session, can help release endorphins, the body's natural stress relievers. These activities improve overall physical health and promote mental clarity and emotional resilience. Setting a routine that includes exercise several times a week can create a natural buffer against stress, helping you approach potentially anxiety-inducing situations more calmly and confidently.

Mindfulness practices offer another practical avenue for

managing anxiety. Meditation or mindfulness-based stress reduction can teach you to anchor yourself in the present moment, observing thoughts and feelings without judgment. This practice can be particularly beneficial for breaking the cycle of anxiety that often accompanies dyslexia, where worries about past failures or future challenges can overwhelm the present moment. By training your mind to stay focused on the here and now, mindfulness can reduce the tendency to ruminate on errors or anticipate adverse outcomes, thus easing anxiety's grip.

VISUAL ELEMENT: **Relaxation Techniques Infographic**

Deep Breathing: Visual steps to perform deep breathing, illustrating the inhalation and exhalation process.

Progressive Muscle Relaxation: A diagram showing which muscle groups tense and relax sequentially.

Guided Imagery: A simple flowchart on practicing guided imagery, with prompts to visualize a peaceful scene.

Building a positive self-image involves shifting focus from your challenges to celebrating your strengths. Dyslexia, despite its challenges, often comes with unique strengths such as creative problem-solving, big-picture thinking, and empathetic communication. Regularly reflecting on and celebrating these abilities can help shift your self-perception from someone struggling with learning differences to someone endowed with unique capabilities. Creating a "success journal" where you record all your achievements, no matter how small, can serve as a tangible reminder of your strengths and successes, boosting confidence and self-esteem.

Finally, seeking professional help when anxiety feels

overwhelming is a critical step. Therapists, especially those experienced with learning differences, can provide personalized strategies to manage stress effectively. They can support developing coping strategies tailored to your specific experiences and needs. Engaging with a therapist can not only help alleviate anxiety but also equip you with tools to navigate both academic and professional landscapes with greater ease and confidence.

By embracing these strategies and acknowledging the need for tailored support, you can transform anxiety from a barrier into a manageable aspect of your life, allowing you to engage with challenges from a place of strength and resilience.

8.3 The Power of Peer Support: Finding and Building a Community

In navigating the complexities of dyslexia, one of the most uplifting resources can be found not in textbooks or online tutorials but in the company of others who share similar experiences. Peer support, the camaraderie found in groups or with individuals facing similar challenges, offers a unique spectrum of benefits that can profoundly impact your emotional and practical handling of dyslexia. This support isn't just about finding people who understand what it means to misread a word or struggle with writing—it's about connecting on a deeper level, where shared experiences foster a sense of belonging and mutual encouragement.

The benefits of engaging in peer support groups are multifaceted. Firstly, these groups provide emotional sustenance. Knowing you are not alone in your experiences can be incredibly reassuring. The mutual understanding within such groups creates a safe space where you can express your frustrations and challenges without fear of judgment. This environment fosters mutual encouragement, where members uplift one another during moments of doubt or difficulty, celebrating each other's successes no matter how small. On a more practical level, these groups often become treasure troves of strategies and tips. What works for one person might be a revelation for another, turning shared knowledge into a powerful toolkit against common dyslexic challenges.

Finding the right support group, however, can sometimes feel daunting. Start by exploring local and online options. Many communities offer groups through schools, libraries, or community centers. These are often listed on local council websites or community boards. If face-to-face meetings are challenging to attend, online forums and social media groups offer an accessible alternative. There are websites that host myriad groups with highly specific discussions (such as navigating workplace challenges with dyslexia) to more general support and encouragement. When selecting a group, consider the tone and activity level of interactions. Some groups might focus more on emotional support, while others might prioritize the exchange of coping strategies and resources.

Creating your own peer support network can also be a fulfilling way to meet your specific needs and those of others within your community. If existing groups do not meet your expectations or if there's a lack of resources in your area, starting a group can be a rewarding initiative. Begin by defining the group's focus—whether it's a casual meet-up for parents of dyslexic children, a more structured group for adults navigating professional landscapes, or an online group that discusses the latest research and strategies. Use local community boards, social media platforms, and word of mouth to invite others to join. Setting a regular schedule for meetings, whether online or in-person, and planning engaging agendas can help maintain momentum and ensure the group provides consistent value to its members.

Encouraging the sharing of experiences and strategies within these groups can significantly enhance their effectiveness. Consider incorporating activities like 'strategy swaps,' where members present a coping strategy they have found helpful, or 'story shares,' where personal stories illustrate challenges and victories. These activities stimulate discussion and enhance the group's resource pool. They allow members to see practical examples of managing dyslexia effectively, fostering a proactive and resourceful approach to common challenges.

In cultivating such a community, you contribute to a culture of openness and mutual support where every member can feel empowered. This empowerment comes from knowing that each shared story and each exchanged tip weaves a stronger safety net, ensuring that no one has to face the challenges of dyslexia alone. Through these connections, peer support groups not only provide comfort and practical help but also transform individual struggles into collective strength, reminding us that together, we can navigate the complexities of dyslexia with confidence and grace.

9

ADVANCED LEARNING STRATEGIES

I magine piecing together a complex puzzle, where each piece represents a snippet of knowledge and skill you've acquired. The picture that emerges is uniquely yours, shaped by how you've arranged these pieces to best reflect your understanding and capabilities. This is the essence of mastery learning, a strategy that, especially for someone with dyslexia, transforms the educational landscape from daunting to navigable, turning learning into a personalized and deeply rewarding process.

9.1 Mastery Learning: Setting Personal Goals

Defining Mastery Learning

Mastery learning isn't just about acquiring knowledge; it's about fully understanding a subject or skill before moving on to the next challenge. This approach breaks from traditional education models that often push students forward to new topics before they've fully grasped earlier material, leading to gaps in knowledge that can widen over time. For dyslexic learners, mastery learning is particularly crucial as it aligns with the need for a more profound processing time and the utilization of different learning modalities. At its core, mastery learning is rooted in the belief that all students can reach their learning goals, given enough time and the right kind of instruction. It's about setting a high standard of learning and ensuring consistent, tailored support until that standard is met. This method fosters a thorough understanding of material and boosts confidence, as learners see tangible proof of their abilities as they master each concept.

GOAL-SETTING TECHNIQUES

Setting achievable, personalized learning goals is pivotal in mastery learning. Start by identifying your strengths and interests. For instance, if you have a strong visual memory and a passion for history, you might aim to master the timeline of significant events using visual aids like timelines or storyboards. Goals should be specific, measurable, achievable, relevant, and time-bound (SMART). For example, rather than a vague goal like "improve math skills," a SMART goal would be, "Learn to solve algebraic equations with 90% accuracy by the end of the month." Break these goals into smaller sub-goals, making them more manageable and less overwhelming. This granularity makes the process less daunting and provides regular moments of achievement that can motivate you to continue.

FEEDBACK AND ADJUSTMENTS

Continuous feedback is the compass that guides the

mastery learning process, helping you navigate through areas of difficulty and adjust your learning path as needed. This might involve regular assessments and one-on-one sessions with teachers to discuss progress and tackle areas of difficulty in a classroom setting. For self-learners, this could look like using educational apps that provide instant feedback on quizzes and exercises. The key is to use this feedback constructively; view it as a tool for growth rather than a judgment of your abilities. Reflect on feedback to understand where you excel and where you struggle. This reflection will inform the necessary adjustments to your study methods or goals. For instance, if you're not retaining information as well as you'd like, you might experiment with different study methods, such as integrating more sensory learning tools or adjusting your study schedule to include shorter, more frequent sessions.

Case Studies

Consider the story of Michael, a high school student with dyslexia who struggled with language arts. By embracing the principles of mastery learning, Michael and his educators set a series of personalized goals focused on enhancing his reading comprehension and writing skills. Regular feedback sessions helped identify that Michael benefited significantly from audio books and writing his thoughts in graphic organizers. Adjustments were made to his learning plan to incorporate these tools regularly. Over the course of the year, not only did Michael's grades improve, but his confidence soared as he mastered each component of his language arts curriculum.

Another inspiring example is Sarah, a college student

studying biology. Sarah used mastery learning to tackle complex scientific concepts that initially seemed insurmountable. By setting clear, manageable goals for each module and seeking regular feedback from her professors, she was able to identify that she learned best through hands-on experiments and visual aids rather than traditional lecture-based classes. This insight allowed her to adjust her study habits and seek out additional resources, such as video tutorials and interactive simulations, which played to her strengths.

These stories underscore the transformative potential of mastery learning, particularly for dyslexic learners. By setting personalized goals, actively using feedback, and making informed adjustments, mastery learning enhances academic achievement and empowers learners to understand and leverage their unique learning styles. This approach demystifies learning and celebrates it, turning every educational challenge into an opportunity to grow and excel.

9.2 Critical Thinking and Dyslexia: Developing Analytical Skills

Understanding the intricate tapestry of critical thinking can be likened to assembling a complex puzzle where each piece represents a skill or knowledge area. For individuals with dyslexia, who often exhibit unique perspectives and innovative thinking processes, this assembly can reveal a richly detailed picture that showcases their inherent analytical strengths. Dyslexic thinkers excel in connecting disparate ideas, recognizing patterns, and thinking in visual-spatial terms. These capabilities lend themselves remarkably well to critical thinking, which involves analysis, evaluation, and synthesis of information to form a reasoned judgment.

To further cultivate these natural analytical strengths, consider engaging in activities that require systematic problem-solving and logical reasoning. Strategy games like chess, or even coding challenges can be particularly beneficial. These activities compel you to think several steps ahead, anticipate outcomes, and develop strategies—all crucial components of critical thinking. Additionally, engaging with interactive learning platforms that simulate real-world problems can provide a dynamic environment to practice and hone these skills. These platforms often present scenarios that require critical decision-making, offering immediate feedback and the opportunity to see the direct consequences of your analytical choices, thus reinforcing learning in a practical, impactful manner.

Beyond games and simulations, structured debate and discussion forums are another effective strategy to enhance critical thinking. Participating in or even observing debates can be incredibly beneficial. Debates require you to consider various viewpoints, construct coherent arguments, and respond to counterarguments on the fly. This not only sharpens your ability to think critically but also improves your capacity to articulate thoughts clearly and persuasively. Consider joining clubs or groups that focus on debate or public speaking in educational or professional settings. The structured, supportive environment of these groups provides a safe space to experiment with expressing complex ideas and receiving constructive feedback, crucial for developing confidence in your analytical abilities.

Applying Critical Thinking in Real Life

Incorporating critical thinking into your daily life can

transform routine decisions into opportunities for improvement and innovation. Start by applying critical thinking to everyday problems, whether figuring out the most efficient route to work or deciding the best way to manage your schedule. Ask yourself questions like, "What is the goal?", "What information do I need?", "What assumptions am I making?", and "What are the potential impacts of this decision?" By routinely questioning and assessing your decisions, you develop a habit of deeper thinking that can extend to more complex life and work scenarios.

In academic environments, apply critical thinking to enhance your study habits. When engaging with new material, don't just passively read or memorize; instead, challenge yourself to summarize key points in your own words, question the validity of the arguments presented, and relate the information to what you already know or real-world applications. This active engagement with material deepens understanding and enhances retention and recall, critical aspects of successful learning.

Professionally, critical thinking is invaluable in identifying areas for improvement, solving workplace problems, and innovating new processes or products. Use your dyslexic advantage to approach problems from unique angles or to synthesize information in novel ways that might not be immediately obvious to others. This ability to think 'outside the box' is highly valued in many fields, particularly in roles that require strategic planning, problem-solving, and innovation.

Encouraging Inquiry and Deep Thinking

Creating an environment that fosters inquiry and deep thinking starts with cultivating curiosity and openness. Encourage yourself and others to ask questions, no matter how trivial they may seem. Teachers and mentors can promote this in educational settings by creating a classroom culture where questions are welcomed and explored, not just answered. This can be achieved through techniques like Socratic questioning, where the focus is on probing deeper into the subject matter through thoughtful questions posed by both the instructor and the students.

At home or in the workplace, maintain an 'idea journal' where you and possibly your peers or family members can jot down questions, ideas, and observations. Regularly review and discuss these entries to explore them further, which can lead to surprising insights and deeper understanding. Additionally, set aside time for regular reflection sessions to review what you've learned and consider questions or topics you want to explore more deeply. This practice reinforces the material and encourages making connections between different areas of knowledge, an essential aspect of critical thinking.

By actively developing and applying critical thinking skills, you can leverage your natural dyslexic advantages to succeed academically and professionally and lead a more examined and fulfilling life. Critical thinking empowers you to navigate the world's complexities with confidence and creativity, turning challenges into opportunities for growth and innovation.

9.3 Experiential Learning: Education Through Doing

Experiential learning, or learning through doing, is particularly beneficial for individuals with dyslexia, as it engages multiple senses that enhance understanding and retention. This hands-on approach aligns perfectly with how dyslexic learners process information best—not through passive listening or rote memorization, but through active engagement and practical application. The benefits of this learning style are manifold. Firstly, it boosts memory retention. When you engage actively with material —through a science experiment, a historical re-enactment, or a graphic design project—you create personal experiences with the subject matter, making it more memorable. Moreover, experiential learning naturally increases engagement. It's one thing to read about a concept and another to apply it in a real-world scenario; the latter not only piques interest but also encourages deeper investigation and learning.

Implementing experiential learning can take various forms across different settings, making it a versatile approach to education and professional development. In classroom settings, teachers can create learning stations where students rotate through activities that allow them to interact with the educational material from different angles. For example, in a lesson about ecosystems, one station could involve assembling a terrarium, another could use VR headsets to explore virtual forests, and a third could involve a game simulating food chains. Each station offers a unique, interactive experience that caters to different learning preferences and reinforces the lesson in a dynamic way.

In the workplace, experiential learning can be equally effective. Employers might set up internships or shadowing programs that allow employees to learn on the job, applying what they have learned in real-time to solve actual problems. This method helps consolidate professional skills and understand the practical implications of their work, enhancing job satisfaction and competency. For dyslexic individuals, who might struggle with traditional training methods that rely heavily on written instructions or passive learning, these opportunities provide a clearer and more engaging path to skill development.

Technology plays a crucial role in enhancing these experiential learning scenarios. For instance, augmented reality (AR) and virtual reality (VR) technologies can create immersive learning environments that simulate real-life situations. For dyslexic learners, who often benefit from visual and kinesthetic learning, these technologies can illustrate complex concepts in a tangible and interactive way. In a classroom learning about human anatomy, for example, AR can overlay an image of the human heart onto a student's surroundings, allowing them to explore the organ from all angles by simply moving around with a tablet. This makes learning more engaging and accessible, as students can see and interact with 3D models that might be difficult to visualize in traditional two-dimensional images.

Success stories from those who have thrived through experiential learning abound and are powerful testaments to its effectiveness. Consider the story of Emma, a dyslexic student who struggled with traditional science classes due to dense textbooks and complex diagrams that were hard to follow. However, when her school introduced a hands-on science lab, her interest and understanding deepened significantly. Through experiments and practical applications of the theories she had struggled to understand through reading alone, she was able to grasp challenging concepts and eventually went on to pursue a career in environmental science.

Another example is Jack, a graphic designer with dyslexia, who benefited immensely from an experiential learning program at his workplace. The program allowed him to work closely with a senior designer who guided him through projects, helping him apply design principles in real client work rather than just learning them theoretically. This hands-on experience improved his design skills and his ability to communicate ideas visually and verbally, a crucial skill in his field.

These examples highlight how experiential learning can transform theoretical knowledge into practical expertise, making learning accessible and enjoyable for dyslexic individuals. By engaging directly with material, students and professionals can overcome some of the challenges posed by traditional learning methods, turning potential obstacles into opportunities for growth and success. Whether through educational activities involving physical interaction with the subject matter, or through workplace initiatives that allow for real-time application of skills, experiential learning is a powerful approach for those with dyslexia, promoting more profound understanding, greater engagement, and more effective retention of knowledge.

9.4 The Role of Physical Exercise in Enhancing Cognitive Skills

Understanding the profound impact of physical exercise on cognitive functions can revolutionize how we approach learning, particularly for individuals with dyslexia. Recent research consistently illuminates how physical activity stimulates brain health and cognitive functions, including areas crucial for learning and memory. These studies reveal that regular physical activity enhances the brain's ability to process information, improves attention, and boosts executive functions like planning and organizing. For dyslexic learners, who often face challenges in these areas, integrating consistent physical exercise into daily routines can be particularly beneficial. The mechanisms behind this improvement involve increasing blood flow to the brain, which delivers oxygen and nutrients vital for brain health, and the release of neurotrophins—proteins that support neuron growth and connections—thereby enhancing the brain's plasticity and ability to learn new information.

Integrating physical exercise into your daily routine need not be a daunting task. It's about finding simple, enjoyable ways to make physical activity a regular part of your day. Start with what you enjoy; whether it's a brisk walk, a jog, dancing, or even vigorous gardening, the key is consistency. For those with a busy schedule, consider short, high-intensity interval training (HIIT) sessions that can be done in under 30 minutes but still offer substantial cognitive benefits. Aim for moderate to vigorous exercise sessions ranging from 20 to 30 minutes most days of the week. Additionally, integrating movement into everyday activities can also be effective. For instance, taking the stairs instead of the elevator, walking or cycling to work, or even standing while reading or working can increase your overall activity levels without requiring dedicated time out of your busy schedule.

The connection between physical health and brain function is a vital element of a holistic approach to learning. This relationship underscores the concept that learning isn't just about mental exercises and intellectual challenges; it's also about maintaining a body that supports and enhances brain function. Physical health through regular exercise contributes to better sleep patterns, reduced stress, and improved mood—all factors that significantly affect cognitive functions and learning efficiency. For dyslexic learners, managing stress and anxiety is especially important as these emotional states can exacerbate learning difficulties. Regular physical activity serves as a natural stress reliever, helping to clear the mind and reduce feelings of anxiety, thereby creating a more conducive state for learning and cognitive processing.

Activities to Try

To effectively enhance cognitive functions through physical exercise, consider activities that raise your heart rate and challenge your coordination, balance, and agility. These activities engage multiple brain areas, increasing their impact on cognitive health. Martial arts, for example, require a high level of coordination and focus, providing both physical exercise and cognitive challenges. Similarly, team sports like soccer or basketball improve physical fitness and enhance social skills and strategic thinking. Activities like yoga and tai chi can improve physical flexibility and mental concentration for a more individual approach. These exercises involve a series of poses and movements coordinated with breathing techniques, enhancing focus, balance, and calm—qualities that are beneficial for effective learning.

Incorporating these exercises into your routine can transform how you approach physical activity, turning it into a fun, rewarding part of your day that boosts your brain power. By engaging regularly in activities that you enjoy and challenge different skills, you improve your physical health and enhance your cognitive abilities, making learning a more enjoyable and successful endeavor. This holistic approach to enhancing cognitive skills through physical exercise not only benefits dyslexic learners but also provides a foundation for lifelong learning and brain health.

As we wrap up this exploration of advanced learning strategies, we've seen how tailored approaches like mastery learning, critical thinking, experiential learning, and physical exercise can significantly enhance the educational experiences of individuals with dyslexia. Each strategy offers unique benefits and, when combined, can provide a comprehensive framework for success in learning and beyond. As we move forward, we'll delve into the creative and practical applications of these strategies, ensuring that the learning journey is about overcoming challenges and embracing opportunities for growth and innovation.

10

CREATIVE AND CAREER SUCCESS

I magine stepping into a vast, vibrant gallery where every painting, sculpture, and installation tells a unique story, a narrative woven from the deep recesses of creative minds. Now, picture that many of these creators share a common thread—a distinctive way of interpreting the world, one characterized by their experiences with dyslexia. This chapter unveils the profound connection between dyslexia and artistic prowess, exploring how traits that may pose challenges in traditional learning environments can catalyze extraordinary creativity and innovation in the arts.

10.1 Dyslexia in the Arts: Harnessing Creative Potential

The world of the arts, with its rich diversity ranging from visual arts and graphic design to performing arts and literature, has long been a haven for individuals who think differently. For many with dyslexia, the conventional confines of textual expression can be challenging, yet their ability to think in vivid images and perceive the world in unusual layers and textures makes the arts a natural fit. Here, the dyslexic mind flourishes, turning perceived limitations into powerful tools for artistic expression.

Exploring Creative Fields

The spectrum of creative fields that welcome dyslexic strengths is broad and varied. In visual arts, dyslexic artists often excel in using color, shape, and form in ways that capture more than just the visual essence of their subjects—they convey emotions and stories. Graphic design, too, is an area where dyslexics can thrive, as it requires the ability to conceptualize complex ideas into visual formats that are both engaging and easy to understand. The performing arts offer another avenue where dyslexics shine, particularly in acting and dance, where strong spatial awareness and the ability to interpret music and movement dynamically come into play.

Leveraging Dyslexic Thinking

The dyslexic way of thinking—which often involves intense visualization, whole-picture thinking, and innovative problem-solving—translates into a substantial asset in creative professions. For instance, in painting or sculpture, the ability to think in 3D and to visualize spatial relationships can lead to the creation of profound art pieces that resonate with audiences on a visceral level. Similarly, in film and theatre, dyslexic individuals often use their heightened sensory perceptions to create deeply immersive worlds that captivate and move audiences.

. . .

Case Studies of Success

Consider the story of a renowned sculptor who, despite his struggles with reading and writing throughout school, found his calling in the tactile, visual world of sculpture. His dyslexia, while a hurdle in academic settings, provided him with a unique perspective on space and form, enabling him to create dynamic sculptures that have been exhibited worldwide. Another inspiring example is a film director known for her evocative storytelling and innovative cinematography, which she credits to her dyslexic thinking patterns, which allow her to visualize entire scenes and camera movements as vividly as if they were unfolding before her eyes.

Resources and Communities

For dyslexic individuals aspiring to careers in the arts, numerous resources and communities exist to support their journey. There are organizations that offer resources specifically tailored for dyslexic creatives, including workshops, networking opportunities, and guidance on navigating professional pathways. Online platforms and social media groups allow dyslexic artists to connect, share their work, and find mentorship. These communities offer practical support and foster a sense of belonging and understanding, reinforcing the idea that dyslexia, when viewed through the right lens, can be a profound artistic advantage.

In embracing the arts, individuals with dyslexia unlock a realm where their natural inclinations toward innovative thinking, problem-solving, and rich sensory processing are accepted and celebrated. The arts do not merely compensate for the challenges dyslexics may face; they provide a platform for these individuals to redefine the narratives of success and to illuminate the world with their unique creative visions. As we continue to explore the intersections of dyslexia and professional success in various fields, it becomes clear that dyslexia is not just a challenge to overcome but a unique lens through which to view and transform the world.

10.2 Entrepreneurship: Thinking Outside the Box

Entrepreneurship is often celebrated as a realm where visionaries and mavericks drive innovation and progress. For individuals with dyslexia, the entrepreneurial path can be particularly appealing. This inclination stems not from a mere desire to be different but from a natural compatibility with the demands and dynamics of entrepreneurship. Dyslexics frequently exhibit an ability to think, innovate, and solve problems creatively, which are at a premium in the entrepreneurial world. These abilities allow dyslexic entrepreneurs to view challenges through a unique lens, often leading to innovative solutions that might elude others.

One of the core strengths dyslexic individuals bring to entrepreneurship is their adeptness at holistic or big-picture thinking. This cognitive style helps connect disparate ideas and spot patterns and opportunities where others see none. For instance, consider a dyslexic entrepreneur who noticed the frustration of consumers with the complicated assembly of household furniture. By reimagining the product with simplicity and user-friendliness in mind, the entrepreneur was able to disrupt a market filled with complex products, introducing an innovative, easy-to-assemble furniture line that catered to a broad audience. This ability to reframe problems and envision innovative solutions is a hallmark of dyslexic thinking that aligns seamlessly with entrepreneurial success.

Despite these natural inclinations towards entrepreneurship, dyslexic individuals face specific hurdles, such as managing detailed administrative tasks or navigating complex bureaucratic processes. Effective strategies to overcome these challenges include delegating tasks that require strong detail orientation or sequential processing—areas where dyslexics might struggle. Delegation not only allows dyslexic entrepreneurs to focus on their strengths, such as strategic thinking and relationship building, but also empowers their teams by placing trust in their specialized skills. Additionally, implementing clear organizational systems and utilizing technology can help manage time effectively. Tools like digital planners and project management software can compensate for potential difficulties with time management and organization, ensuring that deadlines are met and projects move forward smoothly.

Networking and mentorship are invaluable for any entrepreneur, but for those with dyslexia, these resources can be especially crucial. Building a network that understands and appreciates the unique perspective and skills of a dyslexic entrepreneur can open doors to tailored advice, opportunities, and partnerships. Mentorship, particularly from those who either share the experience of dyslexia or recognize its potential advantages, can provide practical business insights, emotional support, and encouragement. These relationships can affirm the value of dyslexic thinking in business contexts, fostering an environment where creative solutions and unconventional strategies are not just accepted but celebrated.

Inspiration can also be drawn from the stories of successful dyslexic entrepreneurs who have carved paths of significant achievement. Take, for example, a tech startup founder whose dyslexia gave her a unique approach to software development. Her ability to think in diverse and creative ways led to creating an innovative app that improved communication for people with speech impairments. Her journey was fraught with challenges, from difficulty securing initial funding due to unconventional pitch methods to navigating a steep learning curve with technical writing. However, her persistence and unique problem-solving approach eventually led to a successful business venture that not only became profitable but also made a substantial impact on people's lives. Another example is a designer who turned his dyslexia into an asset by focusing on visual and spatial aspects of design, leading to a renowned career in graphic design. His firm, known for its innovative and intuitive designs, credits its success to the unique visual thinking processes influenced by his dyslexia.

These stories not only serve as powerful testimonies to the potential of dyslexic entrepreneurs but also provide practical blueprints and encouragement for upcoming entrepreneurs with dyslexia. They highlight that while the path may include unique challenges, the distinct way dyslexic individuals process the world can lead to extraordinary business achievements. Each narrative underscores the importance of embracing one's cognitive style, leveraging individual strengths, and seeking suitable support systems to navigate entrepreneurship's complex yet rewarding landscape.

10.3 Dyslexia in STEM: Unique Approaches to Problem Solving

When exploring the expansive realms of Science, Technology, Engineering, and Mathematics (STEM), one might not immediately link dyslexia with those traditionally focused on rigorous logical processes and detailed accuracy. However, the unique cognitive perspectives of dyslexic thinkers can inject remarkable innovation and creativity into these disciplines. The ability to conceptualize problems from unusual angles allows those with dyslexia to propose solutions that break the mold, often leading to breakthroughs that might elude a typical linear thinker. This chapter sheds light on the symbiotic relationship between dyslexic capabilities and the dynamic demands of STEM fields, illuminating paths where challenges transform into opportunities for pioneering solutions.

STEM fields inherently demand innovation—a quality dyslexic minds are exceptionally equipped to deliver. Their ability to think in multi-dimensional ways allows them to see connections that others might miss, making them invaluable in fields where such linkages can lead to significant technological and scientific advancements. For instance, in engineering, where understanding the spatial relationships and mechanical functions are crucial, dyslexic thinkers often excel. Their innate ability to visualize complex systems in three dimensions can be a critical asset during the conceptualization and problem-solving stages of projects. In technology and computer sciences, where such skills translate into coding and system design, dyslexic professionals often develop groundbreaking software solutions or innovative user interfaces that offer more intuitive user experiences.

In environmental science, a field that requires a holistic understanding of ecosystems and the ability to predict patterns, dyslexics' big-picture thinking becomes an essential strength. They are often adept at foreseeing long-term environmental impacts and developing sustainable solutions to pressing issues. Their unique approach to problem-solving can lead to innovative strategies for conservation and renewable energy technologies that address immediate concerns and offer long-term benefits to global ecosystems.

Supportive technologies have become a cornerstone for dyslexics in STEM, helping bridge the gap between their innovative ideas and the traditional demands of these fields. Software that aids in visualizing data, from computer-aided design (CAD) systems to graphical programming environments that align well with the dyslexic thinking style. Some of these tools translate complex numerical and textual information into visual formats that are easier for dyslexic minds to interpret and manipulate. Additionally, advancements in text-to-speech and speech-to-text technologies facilitate their interaction with textual content, enabling them to engage more effectively with academic literature, programming syntax, and data entry tasks, which might otherwise pose significant challenges.

Navigating educational pathways in STEM presents unique challenges for dyslexic learners, necessitating a thoughtful approach to selecting institutions and programs. Key to this process is identifying educational environments that not only acknowledge the strengths of dyslexic thinkers but actively support their learning style. Prospective students should seek programs that offer resources such as access to assistive technology, opportunities for hands-on learning, and support services that include tutoring and skills workshops. Institutions that foster an inclusive learning environment, highlighted by their proactive approach to embracing diverse learning needs, can significantly enhance the educational experience for dyslexic students, ensuring they have the necessary tools to thrive.

Trailblazers in STEM who have navigated these paths with dyslexia offer inspiring insights and validate the potential of dyslexic thinking. Consider the story of a researcher who revolutionized environmental monitoring techniques by developing a drone-based system that could accurately analyze and predict ecological changes. Despite facing challenges with traditional data analysis methods due to his dyslexia, he leveraged his strong spatial thinking skills and proficiency in visual-based data interpretation to create a system that provided more comprehensive and accessible environmental assessments. Another notable figure is a software developer who, using her exceptional problem-solving skills, created an innovative algorithm that significantly improved data security for online transactions. Her approach, characterized by out-of-the-box thinking, led to developments that are fundamental to secure digital communications.

These individuals highlight the profound impact that dyslexic thinkers can have in STEM fields, proving that the challenges associated with dyslexia can be transformed into exceptional strengths with the proper support and opportunities. As more educational institutions and employers recognize and harness these unique capabilities, the potential for innovation in STEM is boundless, promising a future where dyslexic thinkers are not only participants but leaders in forging new frontiers of scientific and technological advancement.

10.4 Networking and Career Development: Playing to Your Strengths

In the tapestry of professional life, understanding and articulating your unique strengths is not just about self-awareness; it's about shaping the way the world perceives and values you. For individuals with dyslexia, this process is particularly crucial. Your journey in the professional realm should begin with a deep dive into identifying your distinct skills. Dyslexia often endows individuals with exceptional problem-solving abilities, innovative thinking, and a unique perspective on overcoming challenges—highly valued in many professional settings. Start by reflecting on past experiences where these skills have come to the fore. Perhaps you found an unconventional solution to a logistical problem, or you were able to see a project through a unique lens that others appreciated. Recognizing these moments and understanding the skills involved lays the groundwork for communicating your value effectively in the professional world.

Once you clearly grasp your strengths, the next step is learning how to articulate them succinctly and compellingly. This is essential not just for job interviews or performance reviews but also for everyday interactions within your professional circle. Crafting an 'elevator pitch' that encapsulates your unique skills and how they translate into professional advantages can be a powerful tool. This pitch should be concise, memorable, and directly linked to the core strengths you've identified. Practice it until it feels natural, ensuring you can confidently and clearly convey your abilities whenever the opportunity arises.

Building a professional network that recognizes and values your dyslexic talents is another pivotal step. Networking, often perceived as daunting, can actually be a rewarding experience when approached with the right mindset. Focus on finding and connecting with individuals and groups who appreciate diverse thinking styles. Many professional associations and industry groups now champion diversity and inclusion, providing a fertile ground for building connections that matter. Attend conferences, seminars, and workshops that resonate with your professional interests and strengths. These venues are not just for learning; they are prime opportunities for meeting people who can relate to your approach and might need your distinctive skills on their teams.

Furthermore, leveraging online platforms can significantly amplify your networking efforts. Professional social media sites like LinkedIn allow you to showcase your strengths and achievements in a space visited by countless professionals daily. Engage actively by sharing articles, joining discussions, and connecting with thought leaders in your field. Each interaction is a thread in the web of your professional network, which, over time, can lead to opportunities and collaborations that align well with your strengths and career aspirations.

Career development for dyslexic professionals often involves a continuous cycle of learning and skill-building. This might mean pursuing formal qualifications in areas where your dyslexic strengths can shine, such as creative problem-solving or strategic planning courses. However, it also involves less formal but equally important learning pathways like mentorship programs. Finding a mentor who understands the challenges and strengths associated with dyslexia can be transformative. A mentor can provide guidance, advice, and support in navigating the nuances of professional growth and development. They can help you tailor your career path to maximize your strengths and minimize the impact of any challenges you might face.

Personal branding culminates in understanding your strengths, articulating them effectively, and strategically networking. It's about consistently presenting yourself in a way that highlights the positive aspects of your dyslexia. This involves the skills you bring to the table and the unique perspectives you offer. In your communications, whether on social media, in your professional portfolio, or personal interactions, focus on framing your dyslexia as a distinctive advantage that fuels your professional capabilities. Share stories and examples demonstrating how your dyslexic thinking has led to successful outcomes. This approach not only strengthens your personal brand but also challenges common misconceptions about dyslexia, paving the way for greater acceptance and understanding in the professional world.

In wrapping up this exploration into networking and career development, remember that each step you take is not just about personal advancement but about broadening the understanding and appreciation of dyslexic strengths in the professional realm. As you move forward, carry with you the knowledge that your unique perspective is valuable and essential in a world that thrives on diversity and innovation. The next chapter will delve deeper into advocacy and changing perceptions, exploring how you can further influence positive change within and beyond your professional circle.

11

ADVOCACY AND CHANGING PERCEPTIONS

I magine standing at the forefront of a movement, a beacon of hope and change for countless individuals who experience the world through the unique lens of dyslexia. This chapter delves into the vibrant history of dyslexia advocacy, a journey marked by passionate individuals who have turned personal challenges into crusades for educational reform and societal acceptance. Here, you'll discover the milestones that have shaped the landscape of dyslexia advocacy and learn from the triumphs and trials of those who paved the way. As you explore the evolution of this movement, consider how you, too, can contribute to this ongoing story of transformation and understanding.

11.1 The History of Dyslexia Advocacy: Lessons Learned

Evolution of Advocacy

The advocacy for dyslexia has roots that intertwine with the history of understanding human cognition and learning. From the early 20th century, when physicians first began to describe reading difficulties unrelated to intelligence, to the present day, dyslexia advocacy has been one of gradual recognition and acceptance. Initially perceived merely as a peculiar difficulty with reading, the understanding of dyslexia has evolved through decades of scientific research, educational reform, and societal awareness. Key milestones in this advocacy journey include the establishment of the first research centers dedicated to studying dyslexia, the development of specialized educational approaches, and the legal battles fought for the rights of students with dyslexia to receive appropriate educational accommodations. Each of these milestones reflects a growing acknowledgment of dyslexia not just as a challenge to be overcome but as a part of the diverse tapestry of human neurodiversity.

INFLUENTIAL ADVOCATES

Throughout the history of dyslexia advocacy, numerous individuals have stood out for their relentless pursuit of change and unwavering commitment to the dyslexic community. One such advocate was Dr. Samuel Orton, a pioneering neurologist whose work in the mid-20th century laid the foundation for many modern dyslexia interventions. His holistic approach to understanding and teaching dyslexic children continues to influence educational practices today. Another notable figure is Sally Shaywitz, a researcher and co-director of the Yale Center for Dyslexia & Creativity, whose advocacy has significantly contributed to the understanding of dyslexia as a disconnect between intelligence and reading ability. Her efforts have been instrumental in pushing for policies recognizing dyslexia in schools and workplaces, ensuring that individuals receive the support they need to thrive.

Learning from the Past

Reflecting on the history of dyslexia advocacy offers invaluable lessons for current and future efforts. One of the primary lessons is the importance of grounding advocacy in robust scientific research. The legitimacy and effectiveness of advocacy efforts have often hinged on the ability to present concrete evidence about the nature of dyslexia and the effectiveness of proposed interventions. Additionally, the history of dyslexia advocacy underscores the necessity of community engagement and support. Many of the advancements in the recognition and accommodation of dyslexia came about not just through individual effort but through the collective action of families, educators, researchers, and dyslexic individuals themselves. This community-driven approach ensures that advocacy efforts are inclusive and responsive to the needs of those they aim to support.

Challenges and Triumphs

The path of dyslexia advocacy has not been without its challenges. Resistance from educational institutions, misconceptions about the nature of dyslexia, and variability in policy implementation across regions have all posed significant obstacles. However, these challenges have been met with formidable triumphs—increased public awareness through media campaigns, the development of comprehensive support programs in schools, and the establishment of laws that protect the rights of individuals with dyslexia. Each triumph marked a step forward in the advocacy journey and galvanized further action, inspiring a new generation of advocates.

As the dyslexia advocacy movement continues to evolve, it remains a testament to the power of informed, passionate advocacy in driving societal change. The progress made thus far provides a firm foundation for ongoing efforts, promising a future where individuals with dyslexia are fully empowered to unlock their potential. As you turn the pages of this chapter, consider how the lessons from past advocacy can inform and inspire your contributions to this vital cause, whether by raising awareness, supporting educational initiatives, or simply sharing your experiences. The journey of dyslexia advocacy is far from complete, and each of us has a role to play in shaping its future.

11.2 Building Inclusive Communities: Strategies for Schools and Workplaces

Creating environments that truly embrace and support individuals with dyslexia involves a concerted effort across various sectors of society, particularly in educational and professional settings. By fostering inclusive environments, we not only enhance the experience and outcomes for those with dyslexia but also enrich our communities and workplaces with diverse perspectives and skills. The cornerstone of creating such environments lies in understanding the specific needs of dyslexic individuals and implementing thoughtful, evidence-based strategies that address these needs.

Creating an inclusive environment starts with awareness. In schools, this means training educators not only on the challenges dyslexia presents but also on the strengths that dyslexic students bring to the classroom. Workshops and professional development sessions should be regular features of educational training programs, emphasizing inclusive teaching methods catering to various learning styles. For instance, incorporating technology that supports text-to-speech functions can greatly benefit dyslexic learners. Moreover, creating a classroom layout that minimizes distractions can help maintain focus and engagement, which is crucial for students who might struggle with traditional learning setups.

Inclusivity can be fostered in the workplace by adopting flexible work policies that consider the diverse needs of employees with dyslexia. This might include offering software that assists with organization and task management or providing access to quiet workspaces that help minimize stress and enhance concentration. It's also vital that companies cultivate a culture where employees feel comfortable disclosing their dyslexia, confident they will receive the support they need without judgment or bias.

Best practices for inclusion involve a proactive approach to accommodations and support services. In educational settings, this means timely assessments that lead to personalized learning plans tailored to each student's unique needs. These plans might include adjustments such as extended test times, the use of audiobooks, or the option to give oral instead of written responses. Schools should also have a clear process for regularly updating these accommodations, ensuring they evolve in line with students' development and changing needs.

In workplaces, best practices include regular training sessions for all employees to enhance their understanding of neurodiversity and to debunk myths about dyslexia. Such initiatives help build empathy and support within teams, fostering an environment where all employees can thrive. Additionally, implementing mentorship programs where employees with dyslexia can receive guidance and support from more experienced colleagues can be particularly beneficial. These programs not only aid in career development but also help in building confidence and a sense of belonging.

Highlighting case studies from schools and workplaces that have successfully implemented inclusive practices offers practical models and inspiration. One notable example comes from a technology company that introduced a comprehensive program to support neurodiverse employees, including those with dyslexia. The program included:

Specialized training for HR personnel.

The establishment of a peer support network.

Adjusting the recruitment process to ensure it was accessible to individuals with dyslexia.

As a result, the company saw an increase in employee satisfaction and retention rates. It benefited from the unique problem-solving abilities and creativity that neurodiverse employees brought to the team.

Another example is a primary school that transformed its approach to learning by integrating multi-sensory teaching techniques across all classes. This shift was initially prompted by the desire to support dyslexic students but soon proved beneficial for all students, leading to improved engagement and academic performance. The school's commitment to inclusive education was further demonstrated by its parent workshops, which equipped families with strategies to support their children's learning at home.

Guidance for leaders in education and business is crucial in driving the change towards more inclusive environments. Leaders must be knowledgeable about dyslexia and understand inclusivity's legal and ethical implications. They should be encouraged to view inclusion not as a compliance issue but as a strategic advantage leading to increased diversity of thought and innovation. Leaders should be proactive in seeking resources and training and be open to feedback from students and employees on improving inclusivity efforts. By setting a strong example in their commitment to inclusivity, leaders can inspire others within their organizations to follow suit, creating a ripple effect that benefits individuals with dyslexia and the community.

As we reflect on the strategies and insights shared in this chapter, it becomes clear that building inclusive communities in schools and workplaces is beneficial and essential for fostering a society that values and supports all its members, regardless of their learning differences. The efforts to create these environments not only improve the lives of individuals with dyslexia but also enrich our collective human experience, driving innovation and empathy in ways that ultimately benefit us all. As we move forward, let us carry these lessons into our continued journey towards a more inclusive world where every individual has the opportunity to thrive.

12

THE FUTURE OF DYSLEXIA

I magine standing at the brink of a new dawn, where the mysteries of the human mind unravel in ways we never thought possible. This chapter is about peering into the future, equipped with the knowledge and tools shaping the next frontier in dyslexia research and support. As you read, think of yourself as a pioneer in an unfolding story, where each discovery and innovation offers a new piece of the puzzle, bringing us closer to understanding the full spectrum of dyslexic potential and challenges.

12.1 Cutting-Edge Research: What's Next for Dyslexia?

Latest Research Trends

In the ever-evolving landscape of dyslexia research, scientists and educators are pushing boundaries to uncover deeper insights into how dyslexic minds work. Recent trends in neuroscientific studies have started to illuminate the neural pathways involved in dyslexia, revealing that the dyslexic brain exhibits unique strengths in areas like big-picture thinking and problem-solving. These findings are shifting the research focus from mere intervention to a more holistic understanding of dyslexia as part of neurodiversity. Educational interventions are also undergoing a transformation, increasingly influenced by these neuroscientific discoveries. Tailored educational strategies that capitalize on visual learning and experiential learning are proving to be highly effective, leading to an educational paradigm that values diverse learning styles and strengths.

In addition to these trends, interdisciplinary approaches are gaining traction. By integrating insights from psychology, education, and technology, researchers are developing more comprehensive models for diagnosing and supporting dyslexic learners. This synergy enhances our understanding and ensures that interventions are more nuanced and effective, directly addressing the various dimensions of dyslexia.

POTENTIAL BREAKTHROUGHS

Several potential breakthroughs are on the horizon that promise to significantly advance our understanding and support for individuals with dyslexia. One of the most exciting prospects is the development of predictive models that use early behavioral and neurological indicators to identify dyslexia even before traditional symptoms manifest. This early identification could revolutionize intervention approaches, allowing for support systems to be put in place that can dramatically alter educational trajectories.

Another anticipated breakthrough involves customizing learning environments through AI-driven platforms. These platforms could dynamically adapt to the learning styles and needs of dyslexic students, providing real-time adjustments to educational content and methods to optimize learning. Such technology not only supports dyslexic learners but also serves as a tool for educators to better understand and facilitate diverse learning needs.

FUNDING AND SUPPORT

The future of dyslexia research and intervention heavily relies on adequate funding and support. Securing this funding is not just a matter for researchers and institutions; it involves community effort and advocacy. Public awareness campaigns and lobbying for educational grants can play crucial roles in ensuring sustained financial support. Moreover, individuals can contribute by participating in fundraising initiatives or donating to organizations dedicated to dyslexia research and education. Every contribution, no matter the size, fuels the ongoing quest for knowledge and better support systems.

IMPLICATIONS for the Future

Current research trends have profound implications for the future of dyslexia education and support. With a deeper understanding of the neurological underpinnings of dyslexia, educational systems can move towards more personalized and effective teaching methods. This shift not only benefits dyslexic learners but also enriches the educational landscape for all students, promoting an inclusive and adaptive learning environment.

Moreover, as we continue to break down the barriers and stigma associated with dyslexia, we pave the way for a society that accommodates and celebrates neurological diversity. The insights gained from dyslexia research can inform broader educational and occupational practices, promoting a culture where every individual's learning and working styles are respected and nurtured.

As we stand on the threshold of these exciting developments, remember that you are an integral part of this journey. Your experiences, insights, and advocacy contribute to the broader narrative of understanding and supporting dyslexia. With each step forward, we move closer to a world where the full potential of every dyslexic individual can be realized, fostering a society richer in understanding and innovation.

12.2 Future Tech: Innovations on the Horizon for Dyslexia

Imagine stepping into a classroom or workspace where technology understands and adapts to your learning needs, transforming challenges into opportunities for growth and innovation. This vision is not far from reality, thanks to emerging technologies that support dyslexic learners. One of the most promising developments is AI-driven tutoring systems. These systems use artificial intelligence to create personalized learning experiences, adapting in real time to the needs of each student. For individuals with dyslexia, this could mean a learning environment that emphasizes visual learning, offers repeated practice in areas of difficulty and progresses at the ideal pace for the learner. AI tutors could also provide:

Immediate feedback.

A crucial element for effective learning.

Ensuring that dyslexic students understand concepts before moving on to more complex material.

Another exciting technological advancement is the development of advanced text-to-speech platforms. While text-to-speech technology is not new, recent innovations have significantly enhanced its effectiveness and usability. Future iterations are expected to offer more natural voices, greater accuracy in reading complex texts, and integration into various applications, from digital books to web browsers. For dyslexic individuals, this means greater independence and ease in accessing written information, whether for learning, work, or pleasure. These platforms can transform any text into spoken words, breaking down barriers that written content may pose and allowing dyslexic individuals to engage with text in a way that aligns with their strengths.

The role of the tech industry in developing these solutions is crucial. Companies specializing in educational technology, software development, and artificial intelligence are at the forefront of creating tools that can make a significant difference for dyslexic individuals. However, for these technologies to reach their full potential, it is essential that developers understand the specific challenges and needs associated with dyslexia. Collaboration between tech companies, educational professionals, and the dyslexic community is vital. By working together, they can ensure that the products developed are technically advanced and, genuinely useful and accessible for dyslexic users. This collaboration can also foster innovation, as insights from dyslexic individuals can lead to new features and functionalities that may benefit a broader audience.

Looking ahead, the vision for the future of technology in

supporting dyslexia is one of seamless integration and accessibility. Imagine a world where every digital device, from smartphones to computers to e-readers, comes equipped with built-in support for dyslexia. Features like customizable text display, integrated text-to-speech functionality, and AI-driven content adaptation could be standard, providing dyslexic individuals with the tools they need right out of the box. In educational settings, this technology could allow for truly personalized learning, where dyslexic students receive the specific support they need to thrive alongside their peers. In the workplace, similar technologies could help dyslexic professionals manage written tasks more efficiently, participate fully in communication and collaboration, and showcase their unique strengths more effectively.

The potential for technology to revolutionize learning and daily life for individuals with dyslexia is immense. As we move forward, the focus must be on developing and refining these technologies, ensuring they are accessible to all, and continuing to foster collaboration between the tech industry and the dyslexic community. With these efforts, the future looks bright, not only for those with dyslexia but for all who will benefit from a more inclusive, adaptive approach to technology and learning.

12.3 A Global Perspective: Dyslexia Around the World

As you explore the landscape of dyslexia support and education across the globe, it becomes evident that diverse cultural, educational, and policy frameworks shape the experiences of individuals with dyslexia. In some countries, innovative practices and robust support systems exemplify the potential for empowering those with dyslexia, while in others, the journey towards recognition and adequate support is still unfolding.

For instance, in the United Kingdom, the approach to dyslexia is comprehensive, with legislation and policies in place that mandate support in both educational settings and workplaces. Schools are equipped with resources and trained professionals to identify and support students with dyslexia early in their educational careers. The British Dyslexia Association provides resources, support networks, and advocacy that make the UK a leader in dyslexia support. Contrast this with the situation in many developing countries where dyslexia is often under-recognized and under-diagnosed. In parts of Africa and Asia, limited awareness about dyslexia among educators and the public, coupled with scarce resources, can mean that many children do not receive the support they need to thrive academically and socially.

Turning to Scandinavia, countries like Sweden and Norway are notable for their inclusive education systems emphasizing individual student needs. Swedish schools, for instance, employ special education teachers trained in helping students with dyslexia using technology and tailored teaching methods. This approach not only supports dyslexic students but also integrates their learning experience with the rest of the student body, promoting an inclusive environment from a young age.

In the United States, the variability in how dyslexia is addressed can be seen from one state to another. While federal laws provide certain protections and accommodations for students with dyslexia, the implementation and resources available can vary significantly. Some states have enacted specific dyslexia laws to improve identification and intervention, while others lag behind, offering minimal support. This patchwork approach results in a disparity in the quality of support that students with dyslexia receive, often depending on where they live.

Global advocacy efforts for dyslexia have seen a significant upswing, with organizations such as Dyslexia International and the International Dyslexia Association working tirelessly to raise awareness, promote research, and share best practices across borders. These organizations play a crucial role in advocating for policy changes and providing training and resources that can be adapted to diverse educational and cultural contexts worldwide.

The cultural attitudes towards dyslexia vary dramatically around the globe and significantly impact how individuals with dyslexia are supported and integrated into society. In many Western countries, there is a growing recognition of dyslexia as a learning difference rather than a disability, leading to a more supportive and accommodating approach in educational and professional environments. In contrast, in some parts of the world, a stigma remains associated with learning differences, which can lead to a lack of support and understanding. Efforts to change these perceptions are crucial, as cultural acceptance is often the first step toward comprehensive support and accommodation.

International collaboration has become increasingly important in advancing dyslexia support and research. By sharing insights, innovations, and strategies across countries, educators and policymakers can enhance their approaches to supporting dyslexic individuals. International conferences, joint research initiatives, and shared educational resources are examples of how collaboration can lead to better outcomes for people with dyslexia worldwide. One of the promising areas of collaboration is technology-driven solutions, where advancements made in one country can be adapted and implemented globally, ensuring that innovations benefit a wider audience.

As we look at dyslexia support from a global perspective, it's clear that while progress has been made, there remains a need for continued advocacy, education, and collaboration. Every effort counts, from local school policies to international agreements, in ensuring that individuals with dyslexia have the support they need to succeed. As awareness grows and more countries adopt inclusive and supportive practices, the global dyslexia community moves closer to a future where every individual with dyslexia can reach their full potential.

12.4 Envisioning an Inclusive Future: Creating a World That Understands Dyslexia

Imagine a classroom where every child, regardless of their learning differences, receives the kind of education that addresses their needs and elevates their strengths. This vision for the future of inclusive education aims to transform learning environments so dyslexic learners from early childhood through higher education feel supported and understood. The foundation of this inclusive approach lies in recognizing that each student has unique learning styles and requires tailored educational strategies that go beyond the traditional methods. For dyslexic students, this could mean integrating technology that supports visual learning, providing access to resources like audiobooks and digital text, and training educators to recognize and nurture the diverse talents of their students. Furthermore, educational policies should advocate for assessment flexibility, allowing dyslexic students to showcase their understanding through oral presentations or creative projects instead of standard written exams. By reshaping our educational structures to be more accommodating, we not only enhance the learning experience for dyslexic students but also create a more empathetic and diverse academic community.

Transitioning into the workplace, the vision expands to environments where dyslexic employees are not merely accommodated but truly valued for their unique perspectives and abilities. Future workplaces should be designed with neurodiversity in mind, offering tools and technologies that assist dyslexic professionals in their day-to-day tasks. For instance, organizations could implement software that simplifies reading and organizational tasks or design workspaces that minimize sensory overload, which can be particularly challenging for those with dyslexia. Moreover, fostering a corporate culture that encourages openness about neurodiversity can lead to greater innovation. When dyslexic individuals can express their unique ways of problem-solving and creative thinking, businesses can benefit from solutions that might not emerge from conventional thinking patterns. This sort of environment not only supports dyslexic employees but also sends a powerful message about the value of diversity and inclusion in driving business success.

However, achieving this vision requires a significant shift in societal attitudes towards dyslexia. Historically viewed as a deficit, dyslexia must be recognized and celebrated as a difference that can offer substantial advantages in various contexts. This shift can be catalyzed by widespread educational campaigns that inform the public about the true nature of dyslexia, highlighting stories of individuals who have leveraged their dyslexic strengths to achieve success in various fields. Media representation plays a crucial role here, portraying dyslexic characters in literature, film, and television in a respectful, accurate, and empowering way. By changing the narrative around dyslexia from one of limitations to one of potential, society can reduce the stigma and foster an environment where individuals feel empowered to seek support and share their experiences.

To contribute to this evolving landscape, there are actionable steps you can take to foster a more inclusive and understanding world for individuals with dyslexia. Start by advocating for changes in your local school and workplace policies to include better support systems for dyslexic individuals. You can also support or volunteer at organizations that focus on dyslexia, helping them to raise awareness and funds. Educating yourself and others about dyslexia, attending workshops, and sharing information can make a significant difference. Each action, no matter how small, contributes to a broader movement towards understanding dyslexia.

As we envision this inclusive future, it becomes clear that the path forward involves a collective effort from individuals, communities, and organizations worldwide. By embracing dyslexia as a valuable aspect of human diversity, we pave the way for a world where every individual's potential can be recognized and nurtured. This chapter imagines such a future and invites you, the reader, to actively participate in creating it. As we close this discussion, let us carry forward the message of inclusion and understanding, ready to open the doors to the next chapter of our collective journey towards embracing diversity in all its forms.

Conclusion

As we draw this enlightening journey to a close, I want to reflect on the transformative path we've traveled together through the pages of this book. We began with a mission to demystify dyslexia, challenging the myths and misconceptions that often cloud our understanding of this unique way of processing the world. From uncovering the neurological underpinnings to celebrating the exceptional strengths in creativity, problem-solving, and entrepreneurship, we've seen how dyslexia is not merely a challenge to overcome but a remarkable advantage in various facets of life.

The key takeaways from our exploration are clear: dyslexia should be recognized not just as a learning difference but as a profound and distinctive strength. This book has strived to provide comprehensive strategies for managing daily tasks, enhancing literacy skills, leveraging cutting-edge technology, and improving social and emotional well-being. Each chapter was crafted to provide you with practical tools and insights to navigate the complexities of dyslexia with confidence and grace.

Advocacy and community have emerged as powerful themes. We've discussed the critical role of advocacy in transforming societal perceptions and the indispensable value of building inclusive communities that embrace and support diverse minds. This collective effort is essential for fostering a society that truly understands and values the contributions of those with dyslexia.

Now, I call on you, the reader, to take these strategies and insights into your own life or to support someone you know with dyslexia. Become an advocate for awareness and inclusion. Share what you've learned with friends, family, and colleagues. Every conversation you have can plant a seed of understanding and can contribute to changing the world for the better.

I am optimistic about a future where dyslexia is fully understood, accepted, and valued. A future where the unique advantages of thinking differently are celebrated and where continued research and technological advancements further support individuals with dyslexia. I encourage each of you to contribute to this future, embracing the strengths that come with dyslexia and supporting initiatives that aim to explore and enhance the way we learn and interact.

Thank you for joining me on this journey. Your willingness to explore, learn, and grow in your understanding and acceptance of dyslexia is a powerful testament to your openness and compassion. For those who are eager to delve deeper, I recommend visiting websites like the International Dyslexia Association and exploring tools like the Learning Ally, which provides extensive resources and support for individuals with dyslexia.

In closing, I share this personal note of hope and solidarity: may this book serve as a beacon of comfort, inspiration, and practical guidance for all who navigate the world of dyslexia. Remember, you are not alone. A vast, vibrant community is ready to support you at every step of the way. Let's continue to advocate, educate, and celebrate the extraordinary abilities and potential of those with dyslexia.

With heartfelt gratitude and encouragement, Adam Mizda

REFERENCES

Dyslexia Myths and Facts https://dyslexiahelp.umich.edu/dyslexics/learn-about-dyslexia/what-is-dyslexia/dyslexia-myths-and-facts

Dyslexia and the Developing Brain https://magazine.hms.harvard.edu/articles/dyslexia-and-developing-brain

Signs of dyslexia (Primary school age) https://www.bdadyslexia.org.uk/advice/children/is-my-child-dyslexic/signs-of-dyslexia-primary-age

Success Stories - Yale Dyslexia https://dyslexia.yale.edu/success-stories/

Why Study Dynamic Visual-Spatial Thinking In Dyslexia ... https://dyslexiaida.org/why-study-dynamic-visual-spatial-thinking-in-dyslexia-qa-with-jeffrey-gilger/

People with dyslexia have 'enhanced abilities', according ... https://www.weforum.org/agenda/2022/07/dyslexia-enhanced-abilities-studies/

Seven dyslexic superpowers https://futurumcareers.com/seven-dyslexic-superpowers

How Dyslexic Thinking Gives Entrepreneurs A Competitive

Edge https://www.forbes.com/sites/alisoncoleman/2023/05/16/
how-dyslexic-thinking-gives-entrepreneurs-a-competitive-
edge/

Talking with Your Child About Dyslexia https://dyslexia.
yale.edu/resources/parents/what-parents-can-do/talking-
with-your-child-about-dyslexia/

How to Foster a Dyslexia Friendly Environment at Home
https://www.linkedin.com/pulse/how-foster-dyslexia-
friendly-environment-home-msl-centre-pte-ltd

504 v IEP - The Dyslexia Initiative https://www.thedyslexi
ainitiative.org/504-v-iep

People with dyslexia have 'enhanced abilities', according to ...
https://www.weforum.org/agenda/2022/07/dyslexia-
enhanced-abilities-studies/

Multisensory Teaching For Dyslexia | LDAU https://www.
ldau.org/multisensory-teaching-for-dyslexia

Dyslexia Reading Program - All About Learning Press https://
www.allaboutlearningpress.com/dyslexia-reading-program/

Accommodations for Students with Dyslexia https://dyslexi
aida.org/accommodations-for-students-with-dyslexia/

Teaching Strategies for Students with Dyslexia https://soeon
line.american.edu/blog/teaching-strategies-students-with-
dyslexia/

Apps for Dyslexia https://www.dyslexia-reading-well.com/
apps-for-dyslexia.html

Text to speech for dyslexia: What you need to know https://
speechify.com/blog/text-to-speech-dyslexia/

Job Accommodations for People with Learning Disabilities
https://www.ldonline.org/ld-topics/transition-school-work/
job-accommodations-people-learning-disabilities

Creating dyslexia friendly resources https://www.

bdadyslexia.org.uk/advice/educators/teaching-for-neurodi
versity/creating-dyslexia-friendly-resources

Dyslexia reading strategies for students https://www.
readandspell.com/us/dyslexia-reading-strategies

The Best Assistive Technology for Dyslexics https://www.
wired.com/story/the-best-assistive-technology-dyslexia/

Dyslexia Reading and Podcast Recommendations https://
www.thesienaschool.org/news/dyslexia-reading-podcast-
recs/

*Understanding How Visual Thinking Strategies Support
Dyslexic Learning* https://www.inspiration-at.com/under
standing-how-visual-thinking-strategies-support-dyslexic-
learning/

Text to speech for dyslexia: What you need to know https://
speechify.com/blog/text-to-speech-dyslexia/

Apps for Dyslexia and Learning Disabilities https://dyslexia
help.umich.edu/tools/apps

Stay Organized & Manage Your Time https://dyslexiahelp.
umich.edu/tools/tips-organization-time-management

*Accommodating Students with Dyslexia in All Classroom
Settings* https://www.readingrockets.org/topics/dyslexia/arti
cles/accommodating-students-dyslexia-all-classroom-
settings

Social and Emotional Problems Related to Dyslexia https://
www.ldonline.org/ld-topics/reading-dyslexia/social-and-
emotional-problems-related-dyslexia

The Dyslexia-Stress-Anxiety Connection https://dyslexiaida.
org/the-dyslexia-stress-anxiety-connection/

Digital Self-Help Groups for College Students with Dyslexia
https://files.eric.ed.gov/fulltext/EJ1379971.pdf

Teaching Kids With Dyslexia the Vital Skill of Self-Advocacy https://homeschoolingwithdyslexia.com/teaching-kids-dyslexia-vital-skill-self-advocacy/

Teaching to Mastery with the Dyslexic Student - Amplio Learning   https://ampliolearning.com/blog/teaching-to-mastery-with-the-dyslexic-student/

Real World Learning https://dyslexia.yale.edu/resources/educators/school-culture/real-world-learning/

A Scoping Review on Movement, Neurobiology and ... https://www.ncbi.nlm.nih.gov/pmc/articles/PMC9966639/

The Many Strengths of Dyslexics - Dyslexia Help https://dyslexiahelp.umich.edu/dyslexics/learn-about-dyslexia/what-is-dyslexia/the-many-strengths-of-dyslexics

Visual and Fine Artists - Dyslexia Help - University of Michigan   https://dyslexiahelp.umich.edu/success-stories/visual-and-fine-artists

How Dyslexic Thinking Gives Entrepreneurs A Competitive Edge https://www.forbes.com/sites/alisoncoleman/2023/05/16/how-dyslexic-thinking-gives-entrepreneurs-a-competitive-edge/

Dyslexia and STEM - Landmark College https://www.landmark.edu/research-training/newsletter/dyslexia-and-stem#:~:text=In%20fact%2C%20there%20is%20growing,significantly%20underrepresented%20in%20STEM%20fields.

Tips and Strategies for Working with Dyslexia https://hbr.org/2022/11/tips-and-strategies-for-working-with-dyslexia

A Timeline of Dyslexia Awareness https://www.succeedwithdyslexia.org/blog/a-timeline-of-dyslexia-awareness/

Iconic Women who Fought for Learning Disabled ... - LDRFA https://www.ldrfa.org/women-who-fought-for-learning-disabled-dyslexic-rights/

Success Stories https://dyslexiaida.org/success-stories-2/

fostering inclusion for individuals with dyslexia https:// glean.co/blog/dyslexia-in-the-workplace

2023 Dyslexia Research Updates https://www.carnegielearn ing.com/blog/2023-dyslexia-research-updates/

The Best Assistive Technology for Dyslexics https://www. wired.com/story/the-best-assistive-technology-dyslexia/

(PDF) Dyslexia Around the World: A Snapshot https://www. researchgate.net/publication/338910143_Dyslexi a_Around_the_World_A_Snapshot

Instructional Strategies for Dyslexia in the Inclusive Classroom https://teachercertification.com/classroom-accommoda tions-strategies-dyslexia/